The Rural Life *of* England

The Rural Life *of* ENGLAND

By Capt. Mayne Reid

Transcribed, edited and introduced by

STEVEN R. BUTLER
Author of:
Away O'er the Waves: The Transatlantic Life & Literature of Captain Mayne Reid.

Poor Scholar Publications
Richardson, Texas

Poor Scholar Publications

A Brief Biography of Capt. Mayne Reid and Introduction
Copyright © 2017 by Steven R. Butler.
All rights reserved.

ISBN 978-0-9981526-3-9

For information about this and other Poor Scholar titles, please visit:
www.watermelon-kid.com/poorscholar/psp.htm

Additional copies of this book are available from:
Amazon.com and other online stores

Title page illustration from *The Illustrated London News*, August 29, 1846.

For David with thanks

Contents

A Brief Biography of Capt. Mayne Reid	ix
Introduction	xiii
1: The County, the Parish and the Squire	1
2: The Parson	9
3: The Farmer	17
4: The Farm Laborer	25
5: The Ploughman, the Waggoner and the Shepherd	31
6: The Thatcher, the Drainer and the Sheep-Shearer	39
7: The Mole-Catcher and the Rat-Catcher	45
8: Bark-Strippers, Hurdle-Makers and Charcoal Burners	51
9: The Gamekeeper	59
10: The Poacher	65
11: County Society	72
12: County Society in Summer	79
13: County Society in Winter	85
14: Hunting and Hounds	93
15: Hunting with Harriers, Beagles, Otterhounds and Greyhounds	101
16: The Representation in Parliament	109
17: The Representation in Parliament (continued)	117
18: School Persecution	125
19: The Sports of the People	133
20: Associate Pastimes	141
21: Other Associate Pastimes	149
22: Markets, Fairs, and "Mop" Fairs	157
23: Public Dinners	167
24: Farm Auction Sales	175
25: The Best Sort of Englishman for America	185
26: Naturalists' Field Clubs and Archaeological Societies	193
Failure of the English Hay Crop (letter)	201

CAPT. MAYNE REID, AGE 53.

Capt. Mayne Reid as he appeared in 1877, about a year after he and his wife took up residence in Herefordshire; from *The Strand Magazine*, July 1891.

A Brief Biography of Capt. Mayne Reid

Capt. Mayne Reid, the son of a Presbyterian minister and one of the nineteenth century's most popular and prolific authors of adventure stories, was born in Ballyroney, County Down, Northern Ireland on April 4, 1818. In his youth, after briefly attending Belfast's Royal Academical Institute, he left home for America.

After arrival in New Orleans in January 1840, Reid worked at a variety of odd jobs before he reportedly "turned his face towards the Red River, up which he went upon two excursions, trading and hunting with Indians."[1] It is alleged that he also accompanied an expedition headed by naturalist John James Audubon and that in 1840 he "joined a body of volunteers who were about to proceed against the Mexican armed band which had invaded Texas."[2] Around 1841-1842, after teaching in a private school in Nashville, Tennessee, the young Irishman tried making a living as an actor in Cincinnati, Ohio.

After realizing a stage career was not his forte, Reid went to Philadelphia, where, as he put it, "my wild wanderings ceased."[3] In 1843 he befriended Edgar Allen Poe. Between 1844 and 1846, both Reid and Poe were regular contributors to *Graham's Magazine*. Occasionally, one of his poems or prose pieces appeared in *Godey's Magazine* under a *nom-de-plume*, "The Poor Scholar."

When the U.S.-Mexican War began in May 1846, Reid was living in Newport, Rhode Island as a correspondent for the *New York Herald*. In September 1846, he went to New York City, where after briefly writing for *The Spirit of the Times*, he joined

---

[1] "Death of Captain Mayne Reid," *The Standard*, London, England, October 24, 1883.
[2] Ibid.
[3] From a letter Lt. Reid wrote to his father in Northern Ireland, from Mexico City, January 20, 1848. See Elizabeth Reid, *Captain Mayne Reid: A Memoir of his Life* (London: Ward & Downey, 1890), 23-26.

the Second regiment of New York Volunteers, with the rank of Second Lieutenant. Together with volunteers from other states, the New Yorkers took part in Gen. Winfield Scott's landing of 10,000 troops at Vera Cruz in March 1847.

Throughout the Central Mexico campaign, Reid also served as a correspondent for the *Spirit of the Times*, writing about his wartime experiences in a series of "Sketches by a Skirmisher." A postwar story, "Scouting Near Vera Cruz," published in *Graham's Magazine* in 1848, was afterward transformed into the opening chapters of his first novel, *The Rifle Rangers*.

After the U.S. Army reached Puebla in the summer of 1847, Reid was involved in an incident in which he killed one of his own men, but owing to extenuating circumstances he was acquitted of any wrongdoing. Later that same summer, he either observed or took part in several battles.

On September 13, 1847 Reid distinguished himself by leading a charge on Chapultepec Castle. Unfortunately, he received a debilitating wound that would never fully heal. Three days after the battle, he was promoted to First Lieutenant

After Mexico City fell to the Americans, Reid recuperated in a convent. During his convalescence, he reportedly became engaged to "Signorina Guadaloupe Rozas, a beautiful lady, daughter of Senator Rozas, and said to be the wealthiest heiress in the Valley of Mexico,"[4] but they were never wed, most likely due to both religious and cultural differences.

For most of the remainder of the U.S. occupation of the Mexican capital, Reid guarded a convent (most likely the same one in which he had recuperated), where the nuns "frequently sent him little delicacies in the shape of sweetmeats, made by their own fair hands, with his initials in comfits on top."[5] He was also well-liked by the monks.

---

[4] *The Daily Union*, Washington, D.C., March 11, 1848.
[5] Elizabeth Reid, 109-110.

In May 1848, following his return to New York, Reid was released from active duty. Afterward, at the Ohio home of a friend, Donn Piatt, Reid wrote his first adventure novel, *War Life: or, The Adventures of a Light Infantry Officer*, which was published in 1849. The title was afterward changed to *The Rifle Rangers*. Reid also wrote a play, "Love's Martyr," which was performed in Philadelphia in 1848.

In June 1849, Reid sailed from New York with volunteers that intended to fight in the Hungarian revolt against Austrian rule. By the time they arrived in Paris, however, the conflict was over. Instead of returning to the United States Reid visited his family in Northern Ireland, and then went to London, where he found a publisher for *The Rifle Rangers*.

Following the success of his first novel, Reid spent the rest of his life composing the adventure novels for which he was most celebrated Many of the first were set in Mexico or the American Southwest and were partly based on the author's own experiences.

Although he did not write exclusively for the youth market, his juvenile books provided him with sufficient income to build a replica of a Mexican hacienda, which he called the "Ranche," in Buckinghamshire.

On August 15, 1854 at Nottingham, Reid married Elizabeth Hyde, the fifteen-year-old daughter of an aristocratic family.

In 1865, following a financial misfortune, Reid and his wife lost their home in Buckinghamshire. After taking up residence in London, a young fan, Charles Ollivant, helped the cash-strapped author avoid bankruptcy by promoting his most recent work, *The Headless Horseman*, Ollivant afterward became Reid's private secretary.

In 1867, the Reids went to live in the United States, first at Newport, Rhode Island, then later New York City, where with Ollivant's assistance, Reid began publishing an unsuccessful youth magazine called *Onward*. In 1869-'70, the author was hospitalized when his old war wound became seriously infected. During this period, he started receiving a modest invalid's pension from the United States government.[6] Following Reid's recovery, he and his wife, together with Charles Ollivant, returned to England.

During most of the final years of his life, Reid and his wife lived on a rented farm near Ross, Hertfordshire, returning to London only a few months before he died on October 21, 1883 at the age of sixty-five.

Reid was buried in London's Kensal Green Cemetery, where an unusual tombstone, decorated with an anchor, a rope, an officer's sword and wrapped with a sculpted anchor chain is inscribed with a quote from his novel The Scalp Hunters: "This is the 'weed prairie'; it is misnamed: It is the Garden of God."[7]

Following Reid's death, his wife Elizabeth drew a U.S.-Mexican War widow's pension until she died on December 29, 1904, also at age sixty-five, and was buried beside her celebrated husband at Kensal Green.

---

[6] Old Wars pension file no. 47454, National Archives, Washington, D.C.
[7] Grave marker, Kensal Green Cemetery, London, England.

Introduction

By Steven R. Butler

The twenty-six letters or articles that make up this book were originally written by Mayne Reid for an American readership during the spring and summer of 1882—a little more than a year before he died. They were published, at weekly intervals, in the *New York Tribune* between April 2 and September 24, 1882. A separate letter, "The Failure of the English Hay Crop," has been included, although it was not a part of the series. To the best of my knowledge, none of these letters or articles have appeared anywhere else in print since their original publication in 1882.

Frogmore as it looked during Capt., Mayne Reid's residence; from *The Strand* magazine, July 1891.

During the time he wrote these letters, Reid and his wife Elizabeth were living at Frogmore (see illustration above), the country home they rented in Herefordshire, not far from the village of Ross-on-Wye and also the English-Welsh border.

A late nineteenth century view of Ross-on-Wye that Capt. Mayne Reid almost certainly would have found familiar; courtesy Library of Congress, Washington, D.C.

As can be seen from the table of contents, Reid's letters, each of which took up about a column and a half (or sometimes more) in *The Tribune*, cover a wide range of topics, about which the celebrated author not only made many factual observations but also frequently ventured his opinions.

One thing that almost immediately becomes quite clear (if one did not know it already), is that Reid was a thorough republican who had little regard for monarchy, the English aristocracy (although he often rubbed shoulders with various lords and ladies),

INTRODUCTION

or the established Church of England. It is apparent too that he had a low opinion of Parliament. as it then existed, as well as laws which in his view were favored the wealthy, powerful classes at the expense of common folk, for whom he seems to have had a great deal of empathy.

Another thing that becomes quite clear immediately is that these letters are very unlike the adventure books for which Reid was best known. Instead of fanciful stories of gallant heroes and beautiful young maidens in need of rescue, we have here instead a thoroughly detailed, almost methodical, series of articles that deal with factual topics about which the author was familiar from his own experiences, the result of several years of residence in rural Herefordshire (although it appears that from time-to-time, he also did some research in order to be sure, or reasonably sure, that what he was saying could be supported by statistics).

Of course, readers of Reid's adventure tales will know that his fictional works often contain several paragraphs of factual material, a recurrent formula that has often made me wonder if Reid missed his calling and that he might have been happier as a teacher or professor than as a writer (although he almost certainly would not have been as financially successful).

During the summer of 2017, thanks to David Mullin (to whom I have dedicated this book), an English friend and fellow Mayne Reid scholar who sought and received permission from the present owners of Frogmore, I not only had the opportunity to visit the rented country estate where the aging author had written these letters (as well as some of his final books and manuscripts) but also the Herefordshire countryside, where David, acting as tour guide, pointed out buildings and scenes with which Reid and his wife were almost certainly familiar. It was this tour of Herefordshire, in fact, that inspired me, upon my return to the United States, to transcribe these articles, so as to make them readily available to the public of both Britain and America again for the first time in one-hundred and thirty-five years!

Although these letters were originally addressed to an American audience and published in an American newspaper, using American punctuation and spelling, I think they will also appeal to an English readership, owing obviously to the subject matter. But no matter on which side of the Atlantic you reside, one thing I think all readers will like is the way that Reid's descriptive writing almost magically transports us back in time, at least in our mind's eye and in our imagination, to the long-ago world of late Victorian England.

So what are you waiting for? Let the journey begin!

I.
The County, the Parish and the Squire.

Original publication date: April 2, 1882.

Many Americans have told me they would like to know more of our English rural life than can be learnt in a harried run through the country. The American visitor to England, usually a sojourner in large cities, or rushing to and from railroads, has little opportunity of becoming acquainted with such life, least of all in London, the realm of King Cockayne, whose subjects are for the most part as ignorant of it as might be the average New-Yorker or Bostonian with that our your own backwoods, and possibly more so. Familiar with this life from having long lived it, I will, with your permission, lay before the readers of THE TRIBUNE such of its scenes, customs and characteristics as I conceive may be new or of interest to them; and for their better comprehension of it I would ask indulgence while giving some rather dry details relating to its political organization which come under the heading of the county.

In England the "county" is a term of important significance, much more so than on your side; and the name of each county, or "shire" as it is differently called, is as familiar to Englishmen as the names of your States are to Americans. Politically, all matters of administration relating specifically to the shires are in the hands of the county magistrates, otherwise called justices of the peace, with the Lord-Lieutenant at their head; he appointing, or what is virtually the same thing, nominating them for appointment by the Lord Chancellor of England; from which source comes his own commission. Thus it will be seen that the people have neither act nor part in county administration, no elective voice, not even a whisper of it. Such excepted matters as are controlled by their votes are confined to the local government of towns and villages—affairs municipal and parochial—but even over most of these the county magistrate, *ex officio*, wields an influence.

The English justices of the peace, the Lords-Lieutenant also, hold office for life, none of them receiving any pay. And as the service entails a considerable amount of labor, with loss of time, it may be thought strange their thus giving it gratuitously. It has its compensations, however, in the honor which the office confers, and the power; though patriotism and a sense of duty may be doubtfully added as influencing motives. Whatever the true motives, it is an office greatly coveted and eagerly sought after; especially by men of the middle classes who have acquired wealth, and are aiming to enter the ranks of the "gentry," into which it gains them admission. Indeed, so much is it regarded by these, that some would even prefer being on the "Commission of the Peace" to having a seat in Parliament; since the latter is often due to a mere caprice of popularity, and may not be permanent, while the former lasts for life. Besides, the one honor comes from above, and has a spice of Royal flavor about it, while the other is but bestowed by the people. now, as the Lord-Lieutenant himself, the grand figurehead of shire administration, is always a titled nobleman or other county magnate, and as a rule either a rank "Tory" or "Whig" with Conservative inclinings, it need hardly be said that the magistrates so appointed are rarely of middle-class belonging. Cases do occur, and more frequently now than in times past; for even the social prejudices of Lords-Lieutenant give way before wealth. But the truly eligible are the large landowners of the gentry class, not excluding some of their poorer relatives who may not own an acre; the clergy (Episcopalian [Church of England] alone); with naval and military officers retired from service, and settled down in the shires. Lawyers are disentitled by reason of their profession; while doctors, though eligible, are rarely justices of the peace, save in remote, out-of-the-way districts where other eligible persons are not to be had. A merchant—even a wealthy one—in the Commission of the Peace were a *rara avis* [rare bird]; while the holding of it by a farmer or Nonconformist [other Protestant] minister is a thing quite unknown.

Of these non-elected and irresponsible layers-down of the law, each county has more or fewer according to its size, population and other necessities; though in this there is no exact symmetry of proportion: many receiving the appointment as much through favor and for distinction's sake as for any duties they may be called upon to discharge. The average county will have two hundred of them, of course scattered all over it. They meet four times a year at "Quarter Sessions," in the shire-hall of the county town, where they spend part of a week in deliberations, both administrative and judicial. But their chief functions are at home in the respective districts, on the "Petty Sessions" Bench, where some of them sit once a week to adjudicate in ordinary cases of dispute; at least two being necessary to give decisions, unless in matters of very minor importance. The county is divided into a number of these Petty Sessions districts, each having its own bench of magistrates, those resident within it; though some occasionally do duty in more than one district voluntarily and by way of relieving one another. The places of meeting are in the towns and villages, but not infrequently in thinly inhabited agricultural neighborhoods a Petty Session bench will hold its sittings in a country or roadside inn centrally situated. As there is often a long journey to the place of sitting, with several hours spent there, it will be seen that the office of an English justice of the peace is no sinecure.

As regards their dispensing of justice, it is generally fair and honorable. Most of them are above petty spites; and when any case comes before them in which one of themselves has personal concern, he retires from the bench while it is under consideration. Still instances of "justice's justice" do occur, and where there is flagrant violation or miscarriage of justice the magistrate guilty of it runs the risk of a Government inquiry into his conduct and removal from the Commission of the Peace. On the part of the people at such times, there is an outcry against the "Great Unpaid," as the county justices are sarcastically called, and a clamor for "stipendiaries"—salaried magistrates who hold office under the general Government—the people having an idea that these administer the law in a fairer and better matter. This is an erroneous assumption, however, since stipendiary magistrates are as liable to giving unfair or mistaken judgement as the others. Besides, were one such appointed to ever Petty Sessions district, with the usual salary of £1,000 to £1,500 per annum, the rates would be so raised as to soon put an end to the unreasoning outcry, with repentance to follow. The people of England are too poor and too heavily taxed for the theory of justice to pay so high for its practice in the dispensation. Parties in dispute pay enough as it is, but with stipendiaries they would have a surfeit of it. So the "Great Unpaid" have their uses, and as things are I hardly know how they could be dispensed with.

From this rough outline sketch of county organization, I pass to the parish. In England there is nothing called a "township," —a term, if I mistake not, originating on your side of the Atlantic—nee "townland," as it is in Ireland. Here the territorial subdivisions of the shire, both for ecclesiastical purposes and matters of local administration, are "parishes," each a unit in itself. They are of different sizes and irregular boundary, even to eccentricity, some of compact rounded form, others oblong with points running peninsula like, and dovetailing into one another, while of not a few there are isolated portions, as islands, altogether outside the parish bounds and with those of another. The same occurs also in certain counties. There is no very clear account of how these tracts came originally to be detached, as they have been so since before the period of parochial history. The usual explanation is, that this division had its origin in property rights of the manorial lords, in connection with tithings for the support of the Church. For the parish boundaries are themselves supposed to be coterminous with those of the ancient manors, and a feudal lord owning a piece of outlying land would give it the same name and place it under like contributions with those of the ancient manors, and a feudal lord owning a piece of outlying land would give it the same name and place it under like contribution as the rest of his property. As it is now, the average parish may be roughly estimated as having an area of say 1,500 aces; its population dependent on circumstances. But whether thickly or sparsely inhabited, it has its church—the church of the State. Other ecclesiastical edifices may be in it, of the Nonconformist kind—Baptists, Methodist, Presbyterian, Congregational or Roman Catholic—and more of these in some districts than in others; but all such are styled "chapels," and by Episcopalians [Anglicans] oft, I am sorry to add, contemptuously. All secular parochial affairs, as the roads and fixing the rates for them, care of the poor, sanitary matters, and the like, were formerly in the hands of the parish church authorities—church wardens and vestry. But some of these are now relegated to district "Boards," comprising several parishes, to which each sends an elected representative. As life in a rural parish, with its various classes, characters and callings, is an epitome of that of the country at large, I will now proceed to give account of it, beginning with him who stands on the topmost round of the social ladder, the Squire. And first I would ask your readers to disassociate this title form that of "Justice of the Peace": which, if I mistake not, is its ordinary meaning on your side of the Atlantic. The English Squire may be, and almost invariable is, a Peace Justice; but that has nothing to do with his being called "Squire." The title has no official signification, and is solely one of courtesy. For all, it is neither borne nor bestowed indiscriminately; and Squires are far from being plenty as blackberries. Again, distinction must be made between those who by right of birth may legally affix the title "Esquire" to their names, as the sons of certain classes of noblemen, with others whose professions gives them such right, as officers in the Army and Navy, barristers and physicians—and the real "Country Squire," or as he is socially known, the "Squire of the parish." Theoretically, there is one in every parish, though there are Squireless parishes in remote districts undesirable for the residence of gentry; not many, however. But a parish with two Squires were as a ship with two captains, or a regiment with two colonels, and where such nominally exist, as is sometimes the case, one or other them must be usurper.

The Squire of the parish is usually its largest land-owner, and of an ancient lineage. He may be in reduced circumstances, and other gentry resident in it may own more acres and be much wealthier than he, still the title is hereditary, and among these there is a tacit understanding with frank concession as to who has the right to hear it. Generally the Squire is "lord of the manor," which gives him certain rights termed "manorial"—those relating to "commons," if there be any in the parish, copy hold tenures, ownership of the game, etc. But neither have these ancient privileges aught to do with his being called Squire; and are merely attachments to the property he may possess, supposing it invested with manorial rights.

It scarce needs telling, that the hard-drinking, fox-hunting Squire of the novels and stage-dramas is no longer in existence, or if here and there such a character be found, he is exceptional, and in most cases a counterfeit assumption. So far from being such, the English country Squire of modern type and times is a man of education and refinement; in most instances a graduate of one of the two great Universities, Oxford and Cambridge, or an alumnus of one of the four or five fashionable high schools. And in his home will be books of the best, with magazines and newspapers—often periodicals of the highest literary and scientific character. He may hunt, or he may not—his sons always do, and sometimes also his daughter—but he has no special predilection for the chase any more than others of his neighbors who have the means and leisure to indulge in it. The parish Squire is sometimes a titled nobleman; but as titles of nobility are scarce, and parishes multitudinous, in the plurality of cases he is a "commoner." Not the less, however, is

THE COUNTY, THE PARISH AND THE SQUIRE

he of highest social rank; many commoners holding their heads as high as some who bear titles, and even higher. For, though themselves untitled, they may be the sons, brothers, cousins or other near kin to those who are.

The Squire of average wealth dwells in a handsome house, a mansion with park and parklike lands surrounding and maintains a retinue of servants in and out of livery. The orthodox number in the male line would be a butler, footman, coachman and groom, with one or two "stable-helpers," while of the other sex there are housekeeper, lady's maid, house and parlormaids, with a cook and staff of subordinates in the kitchen. Outside there are the gamekeeper and his watchers, with the head gardener and his underlings—all these independent of farm and other laborers employed upon the premises.

There are Squires' establishments with double, or more than double, the above strength in the way of servants; where the butler is styled "house steward," with "under footmen," "second coachmen," "under keepers," "second gardeners," and like graduation of rank, with increase in the number of female domestics. And there are others where only a coachman and groom are kept; the latter by a doubling of *métier* occasionally acting as footmen, with the women servants proportionately few. Still it is a Squire's establishment, and however small, takes rank socially with the grandest.

The Squire is a staunch supporter of State and Church, and regular in his attendance at the latter—both himself and his family, by way of setting good example. Inside the sacred precincts his pew is the conspicuous one; by size, situation and better furniture distinguished from all the others. It is known as the "Squire's pew," and in all country churches, where the iconoclastic hand of the renovator has not introduced changes, there is sure to be such. Double it is, curtained and comfortably cushioned, while placed in the best position for hearing. Seeing is deemed of less consequence, since sometimes the curtains are kept close drawn to hinder curious eyes from peering into it. There are country churches in which the Squire's pew is apart from the others, elevated above them, and curtained like a private box in the opera, like this also furnished with couch and easy chairs. I even know of some nearly as large as an ordinary sized sitting-room, with antechamber at the back provided with a looking glass, while in the pew itself is a table, with paper, pens and ink; in short, all the paraphernalia needed for letter writing. Nor are these things there for idle show, but actual service; the owners and occupiers of these sanctified studios using them to answer arrears of correspondence while the parson is prosing away in the pulpit.

II.
The Parson.

Original publication date: April 9, 1882.

In my last letter I gave an outline sketch of the English "Squire," leaving details to be filled in hereafter as he may from time to time appear in the course of this correspondence. Meanwhile let me proceed to give a similar portrait of the Parson.

In England the "Parson" is the parish clergyman—Episcopalian [Anglican], of course. Nonconformist preachers of all kinds being termed "ministers," the title of "clergyman" denied them, and that of "Reverend" given with a grudge—legally they have it not; neither, by law, an ecclesiastical connection with the parish, nor say in its secular affairs. Legislation and adjudication upon these last are done by the parishioners assembled in vestry, their execution being intrusted to two churchwardens, one of whom is elected by the vestry, the other appointed by the clergyman himself, and known as his church-warden. The latter is usually the Squire, or other "gentleman" belonging to the church congregation. Dissenters, however, have the same right of voice and vote in the vestry as other parishioners. In the holding of his office and administration of it, the parson is altogether free of responsibility to the people. He holds it independent of them, and for life, or during good behavior. But he must behave badly indeed to lost it; and then its loss would come through the Bishop, and not by any act or power of the parishioners. As they have no say in making, neither can they unmake him.

The appointment of the Church clergymen to their benefices, or they are more commonly called, "livings," proceeds from various sources. Some are in the gift of the Crown, through the Lord Chancellor; others at the disposal of the Bishops; still others where corporate institutions have the right of bestowal; while of the 13,000 odd livings—the total number in England and Wales—more than half are the property of private individuals, just as much as their houses or lands! These last—named owners or "patrons" of church temporalities, are of every class and kind; though chiefly heads of great houses—titled families—some of whose ancestors owned them by ancient manorial right; while upon others they were bestowed by Henry VIII., being part of the spoils taken from the suppressed monasteries. Many grandees, as the Duke of Bedford, have each a score or two of church livings at their disposal, and can give or sell them to whomsoever they please, unless under entail, as their lands, or other portions of their estates. Independent of these noble proprietors, hundreds, nay thousands of benefices are in the hands of men of every rank and degree; in short, of all who have the money, with the inclination to speculate in them. Scores of "advowsons"—another name for this marketable commodity—are ever in the market, barefacedly advertised in the newspapers, bought and sold like houses, horses or any other merchantable thing. It is not uncommon to see advertisement of church livings in the "George Robins style" painted *couleur-de-rose*; the parish described as having only a few hundred inhabitants—hence the less trouble with the cure of its souls—the rectory or vicarage, as a handsome house with ornamental grounds, the scenery of the neighborhood picturesque, its climate salubrious, and society of the best. If the living be a reversion instead of one to be immediately entered upon, its occupying incumbent is depicted as an aged man—old as the advertiser dares make him, possibly in poor health and feeble—in short, on his last legs! Half a column of such advertisements frequents appears in papers that are the special organs of the Established Church! Of course there is outcry against this shameful traffic—trading in souls, as it were—still it continues, and will continue so long as England's state church stands on her present footing.

Taking advantage of this condition of things, not infrequently a man who has the means knows himself to be saddled with a half-imbecile son, has the latter trained up for the Church, buys him an advowson, and so fixes him for life. It needs only institution by the Bishop or his ordinary; but this the purchaser of the living—thenceforth its *patron*—may demand if no objection can be urged against his appointee on the score of morals.

It will thus be seen that the English parish clergyman has no responsibility to his parishioners, so far as the tenure or conduct of his office is concerned; neither does he feel any. He may hunt, shoot, fish or frolic, and they cannot hinder him. Many do all these things; though more in some districts than in others. For about the morality of "sport," when indulged in by ecclesiastics, public opinion varies in different neighborhoods, according to the inclinings of the community. But there are few localities where it is rigidly condemned, and in most, the "hunting passion" is among the most popular of his reverend brethren, if all else be right about him. Many of this class I myself know to be truly good and amiable men, of otherwise exemplary life, and assiduous in the duties which their office as ministers of the Church entails upon them. But there are others who add to their predilection for the chase frivolities of a less excusable kind—even criminalities—openly living shameful lives, themselves regardless of shame. These, however, are not specially "hunting parsons," and, I am happy to add, neither are they in large numbers, but a small, exceptional minority.

Episcopalian [Anglican] clergymen, as I have already stated are eligible for appointment as Justices of the Peace; and there is no Petty Sessions bench without one or more of them on it. The chosen ones are usually those who hold the large livings and otherwise are of most importance in their districts, or in the eyes of the Lord-Lieutenant. It may seem strange that of all the "great unpaid," these reverend magistrates are the most unpopular. It is a well-known fact, however; nor is the objection to them confined to the common people. I have heard, and often hear, mean of their own rank in life, Episcopalians [Anglicans] too, emphatically make the assertion that "no parson should be in the Commission of the Peace." The reasons for this repugnance are not altogether clear, though one commonly assigned is that the clergy, biased by religious prejudices, and otherwise narrow-minded, are more apt to dispense one-sided justice. It may be that clergymen who are on the bench, or many of them, are amenable to this charge; since these are usually men of ambitious views, as rule rank Tories, and so, likely enough, leaning to undue severity in their judgments. Whatever the reason, it is a recorded fact that for years past the most flagrant cases of "Justices' justice," and the greatest number of them, have had reverend magistrates as the adjudicators!

The parish clergyman is either a "Rector" or a "Vicar," the chief distinction between their titles being that the rector is for life full proprietor of the church living and receives the "great tithes" —that is, all the emolument attached to it; while the vicar holds his benefice vicariously, though for life too, and is paid only a portion of its emoluments—the "small tithes" so-called—the real proprietor ("lay proprietor" or "lay rector") retaining the rest. In some cases, however, vicars also receive the great tithes, and though the title Rector sounds bigger and is more esteemed than that of Vicar, in point of remuneration there is not so much difference between them; socially there is none. There are poor rectors and rich vicars nearly as often as the other way. This leads to a mention of their incomes, which are not, as many people suppose, grossly extravagant. Livings that yield £1,000 per annum are rare, and looked upon as the plums of the church pudding. A few are worth more, some nearly double; but the majority are infinitely less, and a large minority yield the parson, everything included, less than £200 a year. For a great number of them, perhaps the plurality, £250 might be named as an average. Of course there are rich clergymen, with incomes independent of what they derive from their livings, some who keep up high squire style, dwelling in rectorial mansions, and maintaining a retinue of servants. And form the same outside aid there are many others, who are moderately well off. But for those, the great many, who have only the £200 a year—rectory or vicarage, with glebe-lands included—it is a pinched life and a tough struggle to live it comfortably, to say nothing of genteelly. Even in the remotest districts of England, where household commodities are cheapest, £200 a year will barely suffice to keep the roof over a gentleman's head, and the parson must needs play the role of gentleman. When so circumstanced, as he often is, burdened with a family to boot, his out-door establishment is restricted to a pony-carriage, with a boy in nondescript and somewhat shabby livery to attend to it, the indoor domestics being a cook and housemaid. As these clergymen, to become such, have all been at the expense of a university education—a costly affair in England, to say nothing of other difficulties attending it—it may be wondered at, and asked why they should settle down to a career of life so little remunerative, sacrificing, as many of them certainly do, other and better chances. Does it come of religious conviction and inclinings? Nothing of the sort. Such cases there may be, and are, but only as the visits of angels. What then the motive—what the compensation? For compensation there must be, else they would not be wearing black coats, and doing duty as poor country clergymen. The answer to this last question were not the same for all, since all have not entered the service of the Church from the same motives, or with similar aims. Some, a goodly number of them, are of the gentry class, younger and deprived of inheritance by the heartless law of entail, to whom any genteel employment is acceptable, and the Church is all this. The clergy themselves, too, usually have each a son trained up to holy orders, and always so when the livings belong to them. But it is from the middle classes that the clergymen of England's State Church are now chiefly recruited, and every day more and more; their motive being almost as mean as it is easily understandable. The middle-class

Englishman, who has gained wealth and is aspiring to social position, knows that one of the surest stepping-stones, readiest for ascent of the social ladder, is to have a son in the Church. If the father himself is rich, he can purchase an advowson, and make the son either a rector or vicar. But if only of moderate means, and nothing beyond a curacy be obtainable, even this opens to the parvenu family a prospect of introduction to that society they were not born in, but long to become part of. As for the curate himself, he enters it at once; and, though his pay be but £50 per annum, there is a paradise before him, not heavenly, but one altogether earthly, in his becoming rich by matrimony, and so soon after a rector. In almost every parish there is a woman of wealth, often a widow, on the lookout for a husband; and for this alliance none is deemed more eligible, or stands a better chance of effecting it, than he who administers in the Church. Even the uniform of the Army officer, bedizened though it be, takes not precedence of the surplice. The number of young curates aware of such chances, and speculating in them, were the truth known, is anything but inconsiderable.

The respect paid to the parson depends very much on his character as a man, and on how he comports himself. To be popular he must needs do some service beyond that of his Sunday duties in the Church; show interest in the welfare of his parishioners, especially the poorer ones; visit their sick, and contribute something substantial towards their comfort or cure. Many do all this, at the expense of their own limited incomes, while their wives and daughters are active, often zealous, in such administration; as also in the training and education of children. So in the sense of civilizers alone, these parish clergymen are laborers well worthy of their hire; the great drawback being their pay is not voluntary on the part of the people, but a forced contribution to which all must add—as much as any the dissenters who never enter the church, and hate the very sight of it. Still another per cruria is, that these duty-doing parsons are rather the exception than the rule; while some equally assiduous with parochial work make themselves offensive as meddlers in family affairs. There is yet another class of clergymen, though few in numbers, who altogether neglect their parishioners, leaving them, happy-go-lucky, to take care of their Christianity, as of themselves. I know some who do not ever reside in their parishes, but far away; and who never appear in them during the week, but only in their churches on Sunday, to run perfunctorily through the service, then off again on Monday morning by the earliest train! There are moreover parishes where the parson fairly fulfills his duty, whose churches on Sunday present an array of empty pews. I have driven through a country village, on a Sunday morning, while the bells were tolling for church, to see almost every cottage door the owner in week day apparel—the orthodox smock—smoking his pipe with one or two of his confreres, none of them having a thought about entering the sacred edifice. Inside it would be found only the squire, with his family and servants, those of the clergyman himself, and some six or eight "tradesmen" (shopkeepers)with theirs, who by absenting themselves might risk the loss of the squire's or parson's custom. Add to these a half-score aged and decrepit paupers, in receipt of "out-door relief" who must show themselves there or forfeit the charity dole of two shillings and sixpence per week, thrown in the parish clerk, with the sexton, and you have the congregation as it is in many an English country church. The truth is, that England's poorer people, though nominally of the Episcopalian [Anglican] faith, care very little about it, or indeed any other.

It is in such parishes that the Nonconformist clergy have their harvest. Enter a Dissenting chapel, and how the different the scene! There all is earnestness and activity, with a crowd assembled to display it, while the clergyman administering is often a man who can both preach and pray with eloquence far excelling that of the university graduate. It may be less grammatical, but coming direct from the heart, goes home to the hearts of his hearers, carrying with it a conviction far beyond what is produced by the refined, sometimes finical, discourse from the pulpit of the parish church. These Dissenting ministers labor, and have long labored, under grievous social disadvantages. Among high class Episcopalians [Anglicans] it is thought the correct thing to scout and scorn them. Even a Roman Catholic priest takes precedence of them in the consideration of "society"; for there is no danger of his doing anything to level class distinctions, or interfere with ancient privileges, but quite the reverse. But, notwithstanding this petty spite shown against the Nonconformist ministers, and the obloquy cast at them, they are daily gaining ground, both in power and popularity, of late more rapidly than ever, through the scare caused by the encroachments of Ritualism. Instinctively the people know this to be only Roman Catholicism in a new form, with garb little disguised, sometimes not at all. And as the Episcopal [Anglican] clergy, make but feeble efforts to oppose it, leaving the Nonconformists to stand in the breach and do the brunt of the fighting, should victory follow, to these will surely accrue the spoils.

Not since the days of the Long Parliament has England's State Church stood on a foundation as shaky as that under her now. She seems even doomed to tumble, or be pulled down, if the Liberal party in politics hold office for another decade. Failing this, and the Tories again get the ascendant, she may last, with all her privileges and imperfections. Heaven only knows how long.

III.
The Farmer.

Original publication date: April 16, 1882

Having briefly sketched the country squire and parson, I now offer a like outline portrait of him who may be regarded as the typical figure of English rural life, the Farmer. Not as on your side, the English farmer is rarely a freeholder, that is, owning the land he cultivates. If such, he would be called a "yeoman farmer"; but these are few, indeed, in many neighborhoods nonexistent. Even the designation "yeoman" once in common use, is now seldom herd, and then more as a shadowy recalling of the past than any present reality. When bestowed, as it occasionally is, it does not sensibly elevate the bearer above that general, I may say universal, class known as "tenant farmers," who hold their farms by tenancy and pay rent for them. Any social distinction between the two kinds will depend on wealth and other accidents of life, rather than a difference in the mode of tenure on their lands.

I may here mention another class of agriculturists, distinguished as "gentlemen farmers." Most Americans, and many Englishmen too, will very naturally imagine that a "gentleman farmer" is one rich enough to lead the life of a gentleman. Yet such interpretation of the title would be altogether erroneous. Riches have naught to do with it, neither has the cultivation of an extensive acreage. I know some men farming between 1,000 and 2,000 acres, wealthy men too, who are not gentlemen farmers. They may like the name, court it, and occasionally have it given them in a complimentary way, as it is at times loosely bestowed. Still it is not theirs, in the sense usually understood throughout England, where the "gentleman farmer" is simply a gentleman by birth, who has made choice of and follows farming for an occupation. He may not even own the land he tills—often does not, but rents it like others,—nor is the amount of acres any factor as regards his getting the distinctive appellation.

Leaving these exceptional and somewhat visionary titles at one side, I return to the real subject of the letter—the "tenant farmer." He holds under a landowner, his landlord, who may be anybody or anything: Squire, rich clergyman, nobleman, wealthy merchant who has purchased an estate, or, as in many cases, a corporation either temporal or ecclesiastical. The great landed proprietors, however, are mostly grandees of the titled class, a very limited number of whom own three-fourths of all the land in England, and I may add also Scotland and Ireland. The farmer has sometimes a lease of his holding: but generally, and more of late, his tenancy is from year to year, with, on either side, six months' notice to terminate it. The amount of rent, payable in half-yearly instalments, depends on the quality of the land, with its convenience to a market town and other like circumstances. Some farms are rented at £3 the English statute acre; a few even higher; while others, in a different district of the country, will be only £1. The average for fairly productive land may be put at £2 the acre. These *were* the prices some time ago; but now all is changed, and through the present agricultural depression, hundreds, thousands of farms are unoccupied, their owners seeking tenants for them on almost any terms—certainly with rentals much reduced.

English farms are generally of large acreage; if I mistake not larger than Americans suppose them to be. Holdings of 1,000 acres are not uncommon, and there are some of 2,000 or even more. This depends a good deal on the county; farms in the strictly agricultural shires being the largest, and on some these the live and dead stock will be valued at £10,000 or £15,000. On the other hand, there are farms of fifty acres, or even twenty-five, though they are not numerous enough. For small farm holdings and "peasant proprietorship" have been unpopular in England, the powers that be not liking them. Yet are they just the thing England wants, though her people, strange to say, are little aware of it. The landowners do all they can to discourage the practice, preferring to let their land in large tracts and get their rents in a lump sum, with certain other conveniences accruing. Up to the present time they have had their own way about this, the farmers playing into their hands. For if one of these came to grief and had to turn out, there was no fear of his farm lying unoccupied. The farmer bordering upon it was only too ready to take it in, as an addendum to that he already held, at the same or ever an increased rental. In the way of land, the English farmer is as Oliver, "ever asking for more." Never knew I one who, in his own estimation, had enough, and scarce know I one who has not nearly double the quantity he is capable of cultivating as it should be cultivated. I could point to many who, year after years, have large fields lying fallow and unproductive, simply because they lack the strength in hands and horses to crop them at the required time. England's weather is proverbially fickle, and he who has not the means to take advantage of its favoring spells may lose largely by the want of them. Money will nearly always accomplish this—the ready cash to pay laborers' wages and call them up as by drum-beat. But if the money be not there, and a week of fine weather be missed, or sometimes only a single day, there may be no other chance for seed to be got into the ground as it should be, or crop taken off it. From just such cause I have seen £100 worth of hay lying rotten on the meadows of a single farm, and in a season by no means exceptionally unfavorable for hay-making. In point of fact the holders of small farms, not thus handicapped, are they who succeed best, though it be only in a small way. And better is it for them in the end than for those with large ones without the capital to work them. This truth, almost self-evident, is at length beginning to dawn on the perception of the English farmer—not a very acute one. But his present difficulties and necessities have summoned up the strength of his intellect, and should he succeed in mastering the problem—and find out the mistake under which he has long been laboring—then a new state of things will arise; and large farms will be subdivided into small ones, with a separate homestead erected on each. When this comes to pass—if it ever do—your Emigration Commissioners of Castle Garden will have less work on their hands, at least as regards looking after emigrants from England. Taking English farms as they are now, one of 500 acres would not be considered an extraordinarily large one, though above the average. The orthodox average size will be nearer half this, or say 200 acres; and to such, be in understood, are the remarks that follow chiefly confined.

Approaching the homestead of an English farmer, the traveler, if a stranger to the country, will be surprised to see it place in seemingly the very worst spot on the farm, the most inconvenient for its purposes. Nor is this a seeming, but a reality; the site in a majority of cases being against a steep declivity, where there is barely enough level ground to turn a wagon about upon. Why this is I cannot tell, nor can anyone else whom I have consulted on the subject. It is one of those obscure and perverse things whose very perversity courts inquiry while defying explanation. English roads often run straight up the steepest face of a hill, when a slight turn to the right or left would conveniently avoid it. But for this there is an assignable reason; they are on the routes of the ancient "trackways," before wheels came into use, traversed only by the packhorse, and that under saddle. But the farmhouse, hung as it were on the hillside, where it has been hanging for a period beyond memory, is a puzzle even to the archæologist. In itself it is a structure *sui generis*, unlike anything else in the way of dwelling place. The eye encounters a grand array of walls, six to ten feet high, with several red-tiled roofs, sometimes slated, rising above them; one of these being the barn, often big as a town-hall or church. Others of less dimensions are the stable, cow-house and cartsheds, all set around and partially inclosing the farmyard or "folder." This is a large unpaved space, littered all over with straw, in which cattle and cart-horses stand knee-deep. In winter and wet weather it becomes "muck," when the farm laborers, who must needs pass through, walk in it up to their ankles. Outside is the rick-yard, or "rick-fodder," where the eye is feasted on a like prodigality of straw, put to a less profitable use, or rather to no use at all—stacks of it left unthatched, and rotting under the winter's rain! Yet taken to market when in good condition, or offered for sale where it stands, it would command a price of £2 10s. per ton, almost as much as hay. But there is a clause in the farmer's agreement of tenancy which hinders his selling the straw "off the land." It must be consumed on it; and the cottager living close by, who wants a "botting" to bed his pig, or bait his donkey with, cannot get it there, but must often go miles for the commodity, to some other farmer who chances to be a freeholder. This withholding the right to dispose of his straw as he pleases—the reason, to prevent impoverishment of the land—is one of the English farmer's grievances; no slight one either, and may often be the "straw which breaks the camel's back," forcing him into bankruptcy.

In the midst of the farm buildings, or a little to one side of them, is the dwelling itself, inconspicuous, and generally of mean appearance. Enter it, and if a stranger you will be ushered into the parlor, small and fairly well-furnished, though with a somewhat cold, uncomfortable aspect, fires being only kept up in it when there is a guest. But the real abode and common sitting room of the family is the kitchen, a more ample apartment, with tiled or flagged floor, covered by a spread of cocoa-fibre matting. A high-backed "settie," slightly curved in shape, occupies one side of the fireplace, and possibly a stout, heavy arm-chair the other. The common culinary utensils will not be seen here, but in a scullery or smaller kitchen at back, where most of the cooking is also done. Meals are served in the cocoa-carpeted sitting-room, on a table neither splendidly appointed nor luxuriously spread. The American who has read Harriet Martineau and the Howitts (William and Mary) will no doubt imagine that the English farmer fares of the best—old yeomanry style—grand joints of roast beef, venison pasties, plum puddings and the like. All fanciful—authors' fancies. Never was their description of life more unlike its reality; or if it ever was real I can emphatically affirm it is not so now. The farmer's fare may be plenteous, but it is aught but nice, and barely palatable. Plain roasting and boiling are all of the culinary art known to his wife and her one—there is usually only one—female domestic. Among the country people of England there is absolutely nothing that deserves to be called a cuisine. The Scotch and Irish have their "dishes," some of them appetizing and excellent; but with the English it is roast or boiled, chop, steak and rasher of bacon—nothing besides.

As already said, the farmer ordinarily keeps only one female servant, a rough country girl, little trained, and having slight knowledge of household duties in the "genteel" way. Where there is a large family of children, there may be a servant, half house, half nurse-maid. Of men servants, who eat and sleep on the premises, there are none save sometimes a lout of a boy, who has his bed in the "toilet," some such roost over barn, stable or granary. All man service about the place is performed by the farm laborers, who being on board wages, have no residential footing in the establishment. They come to it at 6 a.m. and go away at 6 p.m.; these being their hours in most districts. And as the greater part of the work is done by horses, the men laborers are few; three or four, with a wagoner boy, being thought sufficient for a farm of 200 acres, even with half a dozen mulch cows and a flock of sheep on it. In England men do the milking and though the dairy or butter-maid may still exist, the poetical milkmaid, pretty or plain, is obsolete.

Among English farmers there is no social distinction, save that brought about by wealth; and I may add, little sociability between their families. It is rarely that they put on "best bib and tucker" to visit one another in a friendly way; this occurring only among the near of kin, even then with remarkable unfrequency. Hospitality to those who are now relations, if extended at all, seems to lack that hearty cheerfulness one might expect after reading Harriet Martineau and the Howitts. Nor does the English farmer greatly indulge in amusements of any kind; his wife still less. They have three or four "outings" perhaps in the year, to attend the district races, or tea meetings and fetes connected with the parish school, where they may witness the usual round of rural sports. Once a year, too, the circus spreads its canvas somewhere conveniently near, and nothing like they better than this—especially the children.

Frequently the farmer is a sportsman, takes out a game license, and shoots. Some hunt also, notably the younger ones, many of whom may be seen at every meet of hounds, in top-boots and breeches, riding excellent horses, their "hunting nags" as they call them. Combined with the sport there is another motive underlying—disposal of the aforementioned nags to gentlemen, who may have been pleased with their performance in the field. But though the "hunting farmer" may occasionally profit in this way, it often ends in his contracting idle, even dissipated, habits, and at length coming to grief.

The English farmer seems to find his chief relaxation in attendance at market, which he does once a week, or exceptionally once a fortnight. Every district has its market town, with a weekly market, the alternate one being "stock markets," where pigs, sheep, cattle and ever horses are bought and sold. An auctioneer is generally employed to dispose of them, this being deemed the readiest way. When the sale is over most of the farmers adjourn to the inn or inns, where a *table d'hote* dinner is ready for them—the "ordinary"—usually at eighteen pence per head, drink of course extra. The time was when at these "ordinaries" champagne flowed freely. It would be rare now to hear the popping of a silver-coated cork.

Politically, the English farmer is, as a rule, Conservative, often of the rank Tory type, his politics of course taking their hue from those of his landlord. If the latter be a Liberal, it will almost certainly be of the Whig specialty. Then the tenant may think as he likes, so long as on election day he casts in his vote according to command. And so has he been casting it for more than two centuries, ever since the death of Oliver Cromwell, not only to his own detriment but that of his fellow citizens—in short, to the obstruction of ever measure for freedom and reform. Just now his eyes are being opened, and good may come of it; but their opening is not from any innate sense of right or wrong; instead is due to his own present adversity; and so little creditable to him.

Rich or poor, the English farmer has no position in what is termed "society"—least of all in that called "country society." Were I to meet a farmer at a garden party, county hall, archery gathering or other fashionable assemblage, I should wonder at seeing him there. He never is—never being invited—and yet is he the man of all England's people who has worked and voted for that which keeps up this social exclusiveness—the man who does most, as it were, to forge his own fetters. I am sorry to say such unamiable things about him, but the truth must needs be told.

IV.
The Farm Laborer.

Original publication date: April 22, 1882.

On the lowest round of England's social ladder—if indeed on it at all—is the Farm Laborer. Politically, as socially, he has no status whatever; neither any in an economic sense, his pay being the least in the land, and barely enough to keep body and soul together. Yet is he often a manly, noble fellow, morally and intellectually the equal of those who employ him; aye, often their superior. Between him and them there is little or no difference in breed or blood; only the accident of some money on one side with none at all on the other. But the education, refinement and manners which the possession of means might be supposed to bestow are not marked characteristics of those who in the social scale stand immediately above the farm laborer; while in practical and useful knowledge he is more than on a par with them. Money he has none; nor is he ever likely to have it. Out of twelve shillings a week, or scant three dollars—his wages in most parts of the country—laying by as much as a single sixpence would be a problem to puzzle a miser. For be it understood that they are "board wages," out of which he must maintain himself and family, feed, clothe and keep roof over their heads, besides paying rates and taxes. The poorest proletarian and humblest householder in England is not beneath the notice of the tax-gatherer, nor exempt from his periodical visitations. In giving twelve shillings as the weekly wage of a farm laborer, I put it at its maximum in most parts of the country; for in most places is he only too glad to get this, and thinks himself among the favored ones if he can secure a contract for it throughout the whole year. Unless a first-rate hand, that he is not always able to do; and in many districts ten shillings or even nine is a common scale of payment where it is permanent; less still if he be aged, or otherwise not up to his work. Considering that beef is rarely under 20 cents a pound, mutton about the same, and other sorts of fresh meat still dearer; that bacon of good quality is 18 cents, and flour usually over $2 the bushel; that his cottage of two or three rooms stands him in rent $20 to $25 per annum, it needs little arithmetic to figure up the amount of life's luxury possible to his position. Enough of life's misery is there in it, however, and more than enough, for the worst is not yet told. There may be days of rain, and are, —not infrequently a week of it,—when his wages cease, and want enters his cottage. Or he may be laid up with sickness, a lengthened spell; then the want comes nearer to what might be called famine—a diet of bare bread and water, even in stinted allowance at that! Such cases are by no means rare. In my own neighborhood, comparatively a prosperous one, I hear of them almost every day, and too well know them to exist. Yet this is the merry, happy England of Chauvinistic newspaper writers and bragging orators— men who know as much about the reality of her rural life as they do of that in the moon, or, knowing, falsely represent. To them the condition of farmer or other laborer is of slight concern, and little care they whether he be merry or sad.

The labor he gives in return for the above petty wage is great out of all proportion. His regular hours of work are from 6 a.m. till 6 p.m., a half hour being allowed him for breakfast and a whole one for dinner [lunch]. Unless his cottage chance to be close at hand he does not go home for either meal, the time not permitting it. They are brought with him in his little bag or "pail," and eaten by the ditch side, even in winter; or if working about the farmstead, the repast will be made in the cart shed, barn, or other outbuilding. As to his sitting down to a spread table inside the farmer's house, even the kitchen of it, that is an occurrence of the rarest, and eating at the farmer's own table a thing altogether unknown to him. Poor is the fare he subsists on, the very commonest and cheapest to be procured; at best only bread and boiled bacon, cold of course. He deems himself well off with this, and cannot always get it; often having to fall back upon a "bloater" (salt herring), eaten cold too. But of all the food commodities purchased by him, cheese is his chief staple and stand-by. It goes further for the among of money expended, and many a farm laborer both for breakfast and dinner has naught but this to "kitchen" his bread with. Tea he can only get on his return home after his task is done; and of this he is fond; for notwithstanding the tax on it, it is possibly the most economical and certainly the most luxurious of his meals.

True, in addition to his wages, he has a daily allowance of beer, or in the apple-growing shires of cider. But this counts for nothing in the way of economy, and is in truth rather a loss than gain to him, as it tends toward habits of dissipation. In hay-making and harvest time, if not under annual engagement, his pay is somewhat better; as then he works by the "piece" or job. Mowing he undertakes by the acre; two or more banding together to do the work. The terms are about $1 an acre for cutting meadow grass, and somewhat less for clover. This includes drink, which the scythemen provide for themselves. If they did not, and drank as they customarily do, a very large reduction would have to be made in the price of their piece work. I almost hesitate to name the quantity of beer or cider which an English mower will swallow, lest my statement be deemed an exaggeration. Still it should be made, and I can truthfully affirm that many of them drink each two gallons per diem, and some even more. Cider is usually sold at 15 cents the gallon, and beer, not of best quality, at 20. But when haymaking and harvesting come around, the brewers advertise what they term "harvest beer" at 12 cents the gallon, and some ever as low as 8—sell this stuff, too, in large quantities! Well might one exclaim with Horace, "O dura ilia messorum!" Little better off are these poor men with the cider when the farmer employing them supplies it. He knows a trick, too; and if the harvest beer be, as jocularly terms, only the "washings of the brewer's apron," in like manner, say they, his cider is less the product of the orchard than the horse-pond.

As a good mower can cut an acre of meadow grass in a day, the amount of his earnings is easily reckoned. But it must be remembered that this no ordinary day's work, but hard, almost constant toil, commencing at 4 o'clock in the morning and continued as long as there is light enough to swing the scythe by. If he succeed in making his dollar a day, it is in truth by having done nearly double work; so that his temporary increase of wages is after all due to a proportionately greater amount of labor performed; and often, I may add, to the detriment of his health. The same is the case at harvest time, when reaping succeeds mowing, with a week or two of interval between. As a rule the corn-cutting is also done by piece-work; the laborers employed at it being often strangers to one another, untied in bands under one undertakes the job. At this particular time the sons of Erin, seeking harvest work, penetrate to the most inland districts of England, and may be met trudging along the roads, reaping hooks and "crooks" carried conspicuously on their shoulders, with other belongings in a small bundle beside. They are often accompanied by their wives and children, in gangs like gypsies, their sun-browned skins and not over-clean habiliments telling that they have been living and sleeping *sub fore*, at a the best in barns or under sheds.

But this annual intrusion into the domain of the English farm-laborer is only for a brief period of time; and when so also are his exceptional wages. Autumn on, his work chiefly consists in raising the root crops, and getting them put away in pits or "buries," secure against the advent of the winter frosts. This, however, calls for outside help; indeed, not all of that which the neighborhood can itself supply; and further on in the year there is still less to do, the staff on a 200-acre farm being reduced to its lowest and regular number, two or three men and a boy. Then the laborer out of engagement, who for a month or six weeks has been holding his head high—no blame to him—returns to his normal condition of

THE FARM LABORER

humility, and hat in hand solicits employment—a week's work, or only a day's. Give it to him at the orthodox two shillings wage, and he will look upon you as the bestower of a boon. Every winter scores of these unemployed men present themselves at a gate, absolutely begging for a "bit of a job." At such times, were it not for the coal and iron mines, with occasional "navvy work" on the railroads, I hardly know what these men would do, save go into the workhouse or starve.

I need not say that there are exceptions to this hopeless level of semi-wretchedness, and that many laboring men are content to bear the constant toil if fairly remunerated for it. Not a few get help from their wives, who follow some industry of their own, and when the children grow up they too add something to the maintenance of the family. But until they are thirteen years of age these are the greatest drawback and burden, for up to that time the law requires their attendance at school, and insists upon it in such manner that there is scarce a Petty Sessions sittings without some poor father or mother being fined for infringement of this statute. To many this law is an absolute grievance. Long before a laborer's child reaches the age of thirteen it is able to earn more than its own livelihood, and so could contribute to the support of its parents; and when these are disabled by sickness or otherwise, as is often the case, even this chance of help is withheld from them. The statute, though meant for civilizing purposes, is a mistake, its enforcement often a cruelty; and the magistrates themselves, aware of this, are many of them opposed to it, but *nolens volens* must convict. If this compulsory education were worth the having, one might better excuse the compelling it. But it is worth little or nothing; in many country schools the teachers themselves needing to be taught.

When the laborer's wife is of the thrifty sort, she will add to his earnings by raising poultry and fattening a pig, at both of which industries she can beat the wife of the farmer, notwithstanding heavy odds against her in having to pay retail price for the feed, while the latter has it at first cost. A garden is also a beneficial contributor to the laborer's resources, and when changing residence he has always a special eye to the amount of garden ground attached to the cottage he may be about taking. Rarely is it more than the eighth of an acre; but, more or less, he makes the best of it; not an inch of the soil is there that is not utilized, and as much produce got out of it as it is capable of yielding. The cultivation is done during the laborer's off hours, when returned form the day's work on the farm; and oft may be seen engaged at this extra toil up till the latest gloaming of light.

Such being the condition of the English farm laborer, it may be asked why he submits to it, with wonder at his not running away from it. Why doesn't he better himself by emigrating? The question is answered by asking another. How can he, or could he, emigrate? To scrape together means sufficient—even the bare passage money for carrying himself and belongings across the Atlantic—would call for the hoarding of years, almost a lifetime. It is a task that would daunt the courage and try the strength of a Hercules; indeed, it is well-nigh an impossibility. As well might the sailor attempt to escape from a sinking ship, with no boat to bear him away, as the English farm laborer from his country; for if not actually *adscriptus glebæ*, he is *adscriptus patria*; and, happy or not, must remain in it.

V.
The Ploughman, the Waggoner and the Shepherd.

Original publication date: April 30, 1882.

Among English rural laborers there are several specialties of calling, two or more of them sometimes combined in the same individual; though often each is exclusively practiced by one who excels in it. Permanent attachments to the farm are a ploughman, waggoner, cow-man and shepherd; while connected with its work, but of course not constantly at it, are the rick-thatcher, hedger, drainer and sheer shearer. Other rural industries, apart from agriculture, are mole-trapping and rat-catching; while in wooded districts there are bark-strippers, hurdle-makers and charkers (charcoal burners—all these coming under the category of laboring men. Taking them in the order mentioned, I proceed to give account of the Ploughman.

On farms of large acreage, or those under the operation of gentleman farmers, there is a "bailiff," whose business it is to superintend field operations, look after the laborers and stock—with occasional authority to buy and sell—in short, like the overseer of a plantation in your Southern States. Smaller establishments, unable to afford the expense of such a dignitary, have what is termed a "working bailiff," whose duties are of a singular nature, but who has to "tackle on" and "hoe his row" with the rest of the laborers. Confining my remarks to the average 200-acre farm, upon this the bailiff is non-existent, the ploughman taking his place as the farmer's head or right-hand man. He is usually a personage in the prime of life, and capable of doing all sorts of farm work well; indeed, has his turn at all sorts in their seasons. Generally, however, ploughing fills up the greater part of his time, with the associate operations of harrowing, scuffling, horse-hoeing and rolling. When all these are over he takes to the wagon, or rather returns to it, since on farms of this class, the ploughman and waggoner are one and the same individual. At holding the plough he is an adept—none in any other country surpassing him, if, indeed any be his equal, which I doubt. He will run a furrow lengthwise through a forty-acre field straight as the shaft of a lance, and lay the whole field over in regular parallels, like the ribs on a corduroy web. Withal, the work is slowly done, though that is not his fault, but the fault of the system. An acre a day on fairly level ground is considered a good average, and to plough this tow of the largest horses are employed—in heavy land three—geared tandem-fashion, with a boy the "waggoner's boy" to lead and turn them on the headlands. One of your great steam-ploughing prairie farmers would be tortured to witness such crawling work, and not much wonder. For considering its cost in man's wages and horse-keep, with the selling price of farm produce as it is now in England, the thing poorly pays. Undoubtedly it is one of the factors which hinder English agriculture from being a profitable occupation. We have the steam plough too, of various sorts and specialties, but its employment is exceptional. However well the English ploughman may do his work, his wages are little above those of any other farm hand—two or three shillings a week at the utmost, and often not so much; his chief compensation being in that his engagement is generally permanent,. As already stated, when the ploughing, with other tillage is finished, he resumes his place as The Waggoner.

This role, in point of fact, he has never resigned; since waggoning is done at all times and seasons of the year. In winter and spring the manure has to be distributed over the land, in summer and autumn the hay and corn must be got home to the rick-folder; and again the hay and threshed-out grain must be transported to mill or market. There are journeyings, also, to coal mines and railway stations to fetch coal, not alone for the farmer himself, but frequently in the service of a neighbor, who, not having horse or wagon of his own, has to charter them. The English farm wagon is an immense cumbersome vehicle, of itself a load when empty. Two tons and a half are its ordinary lading, drawn by a couple of gigantic horses—"English elephants" as some astonished Orientals on first seeing pronounced them—or more usually three, which, as in the plough, are attached tandem. Four, five and six are sometimes used in timber hauling or transporting heavy blocks of building stone from the quarries. These, however, are specialties apart from the work of the farm waggoner, and to him we return. He takes great pride in his horses, likes to see them well-conditioned, with their coats glossy; and has a knowledge of all the "balls" and medicaments tending to produce this effect. It pleases him also to have them generally geared, the straps with big brass buckles, a high-pitched housing on the collar, with tinkling bells, and a cockade of scarlet or white horse hair surmounting their frontlets. Still more does the waggoner's boy exult in this luxury of ornamentation, especially when a new hand to the business; and some will voluntarily spend part of their slender earnings in the purchase of a superior kind of whip with brass rings set thick along the stock. This in hand, they think themselves no longer boys.

One peculiarity about English waggoners, which has often surprised, not to say puzzled me, may be worth noting. No matter what their age or natural tone of voice, the peculiar phraseology employed by them in the guidance of their teams—the "come hee'er" and "gee-woat-tha"—that is intoned as much alike as if it all came out of the same throat. Without seeing the man himself, though he may be well-known, it were difficult to identify him by these utterances. No doubt the similarity of tone and pronunciation is attained by imitation, yet is it a remarkable instance of this faculty.

As with ploughman and waggoner, so with cowman and shepherd, these two being commonly one and the same man. Of course there are exceptions on pasture farms where many milch cows are kept. Then they are separate callings; the cow man having full employment in milking and tending the cattle. But on the ordinary tillage farm, where these are few, he becomes merged in The Shepherd.

In the individuals who follow this calling, again, a difference needs to be noted. There are shepherds and shepherds, some more skilled in their craft—for it is a craft—and better paid than others, from having a more important charge, with a larger flock to look after. Many of these men receive even higher wages than a ploughman, and there are perquisites given them, when lambs and dams have been safely carried through the yeaning season, and their owners think this is part due to the watchful care of the shepherd. On most farms, however, sheep-keeping, though one of the industries, is not the chief one; and a flock of from 50 to 100 is all that will be maintained. In these cases the shepherd's wages are no more than those of any other laborer, and often less. For he is often aged and somewhat decrepit—having seen his best days. Still he knows all about sheep and their ways; is learned in their complaints and diseases, which are multifarious; can "dip" to rid them of ticks and other skin troubles; anoint to cure them of the scab and foot rot; though the "flukes" or liver-rot are beyond his skill, as they are beyond that of all others. Most of his time is spent by or near his charge, especially in the winter and spring. During the former they need food more than pasture grass supplies. Then they have to be "penned" in a field of turnips or Swedes; these roots being sometimes forked out of the ground for them, but as often eaten in it. The penning is done with rough wooden hurdles, the field taken in sections successively; as, were the sheep allowed to ramble all over it, they might destroy as much as they would eat. Therefore, putting the hurdles to form fresh inclosures is one of the shepherd's jobs. It requires a crowbar and mallet to lay them firmly; and as these with some other necessary implements and utensils cannot with convenience be diurnally taken to the field and fetched away from it, a wooden house on wheels, like a large sentry-box, is kept in it to give them storage. This also shelters the shepherd himself in severe weather, when it snows or rains. Sometimes the roots are sliced or pulped before being flung to the sheep, and for this purpose a slicer or pulper will be seen close by; the shepherd turning away at the crank when a fresh supply is called for.

Victorian English shepherd; courtesy Library of Congress, Washington, D.C.

The shepherd's every-day dress is the long skirted smock of twilled cotton stuff, closed both at back and breast, and only to got on by pulling it over the head. Elaborately stitched and plaited, this truly rustic costume seems more special to shepherds than to other farm laborers, though many of all sorts cling to it; and when wet it clings to them. Our shepherd also carries the orthodox pastoral "crook," for how could he catch up a sheep when wanted without it? Even with this his chances of doing so would be small were it not for another adjunct, a living one, possessed of intellectuality almost equaling his own—the sheep dog. In the portraiture of an English shepherd to omit delineation of his dog were to leave the picture incomplete. So I ask permission to add this in, as transcribed from a memorandum I lately made relating to a sheep dog in my own possession. Thus runs it, just as jotted down:

I have a sheep dog whose sagacity is truly surprising; he seems up to everything short of articulate speech. But *think* he can, and clearly, as testified by the expression of his eyes, and the display of cunning with capability in his actions. He is of a strain so somewhat remarkable; the bitch, his great-grandam, having borne whelps to a dog fox, one if which was his grandsire. This singular cross occurred among the Welsh mountains, in a wood adjoining the sheep farm where the bitch belonged. The parturition took place in the fox's burrow, inside which the pups were suckled by their dam, and there kept till able to run about. Then these half bred canines were caught and brought home to the farmhouse, the mother following. It was a curious instance of cross-breeding between the tame and the wild; animals, too, so specifically distinct and usually at bitter war with one another; still not unprecedented, many similar cases having been recorded. Whether his semi-vulpine ancestry had done anything to sharpen the wits of my sheep-dog I know not. But there is nothing vulpine in his nature; no fierce ravening instructs, as might be expected from such a strain; instead, he is remarkably gentle and affectionate, and never so happy as when he sees a flock of sheep, and stands awaiting the order to fetch them to the fold or up to the foot of the shepherd. Then his eyes fairly dance with delight, his whole body quivering with anticipated pleasure. On getting the word "go" he is off like an arrow from the bow, or greyhound unleased at a hare. But not with live evil intent; for his treats the ovines tenderly as may be. Necessarily now and then with his snout he bowls over one that is obstinate, and will not run the right way; but near to bit nor tear it. He is up to all sorts of sheep-dog doings, and that is being up to a great deal; since some of these are positively astounding. One which I was witness to the other day furnished as clear evidence of mental ratiocination as could well be. A flock of sheep was being driven along the road with two dogs attendant

THE PLOUGHMAN, THE WAGGONER AND THE SHEPHERD

besides the driver. One of them kept behind the sheep, the other in advance of them, and at each open gate or break in the bordering fences the latter would take stand and stay there as a sentinel on post of guard till the headmost of the flock was fairly up to him, with the certainty of their passing on. Then would the knowing animal start off, and rush ahead again to look out for any other open place there might be along the double line of fencing. Nor was this all; a still greater degree of sagacity on the dog's part remaining to be recorded—a very subtleness of reasoning for to call it instinct were to palter with words. When there was a break or "glat" in the fence doubtfully wide enough to give passage to the body of a sheep, I saw the dog stand regarding it, evidently pondering on the possibilities of the sheep getting through, and at length satisfied they could not, trot on to examine the next opening!

Bob, as my own canine is called, can do all this with the other sheep-dog tricks, and something more; a something I should have been loath to believe had I not actually witnessed it. As all know, the tick is a troublesome pest to the poor sheep, oft irritating them exceedingly; and a good shepherd will now and then do his best endeavor to ride them of the annoyance by picking the insects off. Several times when mine has been so employed have I seen Bob helping him; the dog burying his snout in the sheep's wool, and nosing about till he came upon a tick, and then catching the ugly beast and "scrunching" it between his teeth in the most business-like manner; when he would drop it and proceed in search of another! Nor had anything been done to teach him this; he simply saw the shepherd engaged in removing the ticks and killing them; knew they were something to be destroyed, and so lent his teeth to destroying them. I will make no comment on this curious proceeding further than to say that on witnessing it I was struck with astonishment. Who could have been otherwise? And after that, who is the sceptic to deny to dumb animals the possession of intellect, altogether apart from what is termed instinct?

Thatching; from the *Illustrated London News*, October 3, 1846.

VI.
The Thatcher, the Drainer and the Sheep-Shearer.

Original publication date: May 7, 1882

Continuing my account of English rural laborers I come next to The Rick-Thatcher. His is a specialty of farm-work which calls for considerable skill, and there are men who follow it a s profession during the few weeks of the year while it lasts. Some small farmers thatch their own stacks; and others, who chance to have dexterous hand in their employ, dispense with the services of the regular rick-thatcher. Generally, however, he is called in, and as both hay-ricks and wheat-stacks after being built are necessarily allowed to stand some time, so that they may get "set" before being thatched, the thatcher has an opportunity of undertaking the work on several farms. Having secured his engagements he goes from one to the other in succession, as the ricks become ready to have their winter top-coat put on. A somewhat elaborate affair this is, and rather a costly one; the thatch being of the best wheaten straw, straight drawn, and separated into "handfuls," these laid on, "rodded" and "buckled down," with as much are as though it were the thatching of a house. If the rickyard be alongside or within near view of a public road, extra pains are taken to give everything a trim, tidy appearance, both farmer and thatcher taking a pride in this. The square or oblong-square ricks, usually of hay, will have an elaborate platting along the ridge, while the round ones of wheat, barley or oats show on their summits a cockade-like tuft, sometimes globe-shaped, but more frequently cut to resemble a wine-glass, and bearing that name. The payment for rick-thatching is not by the day, but by the rick or stack, and of course varies according to their size; and as the work is only temporary, wages are high in proportion. Besides, the thatcher is no common farm hand, but a craftsman of skill; usually a man over middle age, sober and steady in habits. Sometimes he is an old man, but from having lived a regular life still keeps hale and strong, in every way up to his work, which, just as with the ploughman, he executes in a superior manner.

When in autumn the thatching season comes to an end, as it necessarily must, he betakes himself to some other calling, which in nine cases out of ten is that of the Hedger—another specialty of England labor requiring skill, knowledge and experience. The "pleaching" of a hedge is an art in itself, which an ordinary farm hand is not up to; a work also which every winter furnishes employment to a goodly number of men for several weeks, or even months. In most parts of England the farm fields are fenced in with hawthorn hedges; the thorns when young and "quick" being planted in a row, along the sloping face of a straight earthen embankment near its crest. They are protected by post and rail till they attain sufficient growth to form a fence of themselves. In the lapse of years their thick branching heads will have gone up some three or four feet above the earthen ridge, which has become dilapidated and between their stoles there will be spaces widen enough to let sheep through. Gaps, in some districts called "glats," will also appear where horses or cattle have taken advantage of a weak place in the hedge, and broken through it. Sometimes, also, the hounds may have swept over the farm, with a ruck of galloping horsemen, making the "glats" wider and worse. To remedy all this and put the fence in proper condition is the work of the hedger, who is now employed to "pleach" the hedge. This he does by hacking the stems of the thorns bending them down, and working them into a wattle around ribs called "hedge-stakes," which he has already driven firmly into the embankment forming the base of the fence. The stems are hacked about two feet above the ridge's crest, and just enough to make them breakable; then they are laid down horizontally, or nearly so, and through crushed continue to grow; the hawthorn being a hardy shrub and difficult to kill. In many hedges the stoles stand too thick to admit of this bending over one another; in which case some are cut clean through, dragged out, and so thinned to requirement. When there are long breaks, as often happens, these are made good by stakes and a wicker of detached branches; but this soon decays and need renewal nearly every year.

A newly "pleached" hedge, when done by a hedger thoroughly up to his work—and few are not up to it—is rather a pleasing sight; the stakes at regular distances apart, their heads on the same level, and the thorns laid symmetrically along them, imparting an idea of strength combined with neatness. No animal will attempt breaking through it then, and still less after spring brings the hawthorns into leaf, making it a solid mass of green.

For tools the hedger has a bill-hook, or rather two of them, one long-handled, the other short; these are the ordinary choppers. The axe is also an adjunct of his calling; but there is yet another equipment, without which he would be ill able to follow it, or only with hands and wrists sorely lacerated. A somewhat costly affair it is, being a pair of sealskin gloves, for which he has to pay four shillings and sixpence—rather more than a dollar—a heavy expenditure for a poor laboring man. But the gloves are essential to his safety, and must be sealskin—no ordinary hid or leather being thorn-proof—and gauntletted. So he pays the four and sixpence, knowing he cannot help himself, but with somewhat of a grimace.

The scale of remuneration for hedge-pleaching is one penny per lineal yard, if the thorns be regular, and not too thick or left standing for too long a time. In these cases, and also when there are frequent breaks in the fence needing to be made good, nearly double the above price has to be paid him, or one shilling the pole of five and a half yards. As his work is neither constant nor permanent, for this reason, while it least, it is more remunerative than ordinary farm labor. But the hedger is rarely out of a job; for when both rick-thatching and pleaching fail him, there is pruning to do in shrubberies and orchards. The former, as must needs be, he undertakes by the day, while the latter is done by the tree; the price charged for pear and apple trees being about threepence each, exclusive "victuals and drink." Having just paid the bill for having my own orchards put in order, I speak from personal knowledge.

Cognate with farm labor, through distinct from it, is the work of The Drainer, this too needing knowledge of a special kind. But it is only in certain districts of country where the land lies low and wet that the drainer is an acknowledged separate entity of the population as regards his calling. There he is looked upon in the light of a craftsman, rather than laborer; for besides hollowing out a trench he must know something about levels, in what direction water will run, how to lay the conduit pipes, and construct culverts. Thus accomplished, his wages are of course far above what are paid the ordinary laborer, and nearly on a par with those of the bricklayer and carpenter.

Still another of the exceptional and temporary employments of English rural life is that of The Sheep-Shearer. His time comes in the spring, generally about the middle of April. Then only the fat sheep are shorn, those destined to death at the hands of the butcher. At this season it is too cold for the ewes that have lambs to go without their winter coats, and not until May are these stripped off them. Frequently the owner of fat sheep, wishing to get them to marker, and so realize on them, has the shearing done at a date earlier than usual. To let the butcher have their wool would be bad economy, and he prefers selling this commodity direct to the "wool-stapler." But in thus depriving the animals of their fleece before the customary time, he must needs be cautious. If the weather chances to be chilly, and the sheep be seen naked by the rural policeman, presto! the farmer, their owner, gets "pulled up"—in other words brought before the magisterial bench—and smartly fined. To avoid this dilemma, the law allows early shearing of fat sheep, but with the proviso that each shall have a warm woolen cloth strapped upon it; and it is no uncommon sight to see a flock of fine wethers driven to market wearing covers like so many high-blooded horses.

Sheep shearing; from the *Illustrated London News*, July 18, 1846.

As with rick-thatching, sometimes the farmer shears his own sheep, or he may have a hired hand dexterous enough to do it. But this is rare; and in nine cases out of ten the professional shearer is called in, bringing his shears and other appliances with him. The flock is driven up to him, either into the "folder" or some other convenient spot, by the shepherd and do, where he falls to and will strip off twenty-five fleeces in a day. This is a good day's work, though there are shearers who will do thirty; while younger and less skilled hands fall short of the score. It is by the score that payment is made; the price being two shillings and sixpence, or about 3 cents per head. But as with the tree-pruner, the shearer of sheep must have "Victuals and drink" in addition, as, providing these for himself, his terms would be somewhat higher. When the shearing season is over he looks out for other work of various kinds. In most cases he is a bit of a butcher and can slaughter a sheep as well as clip it, this furnishing him with an occasional job. He is also a "pig-sticker," which, when the cold weather comes on, and all through the winter, gives him employment, profitable if not constant. For farmers, even poor cottagers, have always pigs to kill and cure their own bacon. In many cases the sheep-shearer is himself a farmer of small holding; and when not called away from it, finds ample occupation in looking after the husbandry of his own limited acreage.

As a rule, all these men do their work wonderfully well, some of them taking great pride in it. And to encourage this, there are competitive trials at nearly all the local or county agricultural shows, with prizes bestowed on the successful competitors.

VII.
The Mole Catcher and the Rat-Catcher.

Original publication date: May 14, 1882.

Among the quaintest of English rural industries is that of mole-catching, which by certain individuals is followed as a regular calling. Every neighborhood where moles abound has its professional Mole-Catcher; though there are districts in which these semi-subterranean quadrupeds are not so plentiful as to need thinning off; tracts of country where the soil, from its geological character, is too poor to produce a thick crop of earthworms—the mole's orthodox diet. To the fauna of Ireland the mole is altogether wanting, for what reason naturalists have never been able to determine. Whether like the snakes, it was excommunicated by St. Patrick, history does not record; but if so, the Saint deserves credit for ridding the Emerald Isle of a pest noxious as the reptiles themselves, if not so dangerous. I may say, however, that about this there is a difference of opinion, many people looking upon the mole as more profit than pest. These are not farmers, though; instead, newspaper writers of the closet-naturalist kind; and every now and then arises discussion on this subject with voluminous correspondence in which the farmer is ridiculed for his ignorance and accused of ingratitude in waging war against *Talpa*, his benefactor! According to these theorists, the mole eats the "wire-worm," Elates lineatus, and so destroys large quantities of these insect larvæ that would otherwise do much injury to the young wheat plant and all sorts of growing produce. In the pursuit of natural history I have taken pains to ascertain the truth about this matter; and after repeated experiments am able to affirm that the farmer is in the right, and those who cast ridicule on him in the wrong. The mole does not and will not eat wire-worm; the common ground worm, Lumbricus terrestris, being its natural food; and, I believe, sole sustenance, or nearly so.

Another slight digression from the chief purpose of this article may be necessary, to say that the mole of England, Talpa Europea, is specifically different from any of the species indigenous to America; and hair-splitting naturalists even make it distinct in genus. It is, however, so closely allied to the common mole of the States, T. Virginiano, in size, appearance, ways, habits and everything that the reader may look upon them as essentially the same.

The greatest damage done by the English mole is to grass, both that of pasture lands and meadows kept for hay. In tunneling after worms, as is well known, it here and there throws up heaps of loose earth, of conical or hemispherical shape—"molehills," so-called—some of which I have measured and found to be over two feel in horizontal diameter, the upheaved earth filling a bushel basket. Such are of exceptional size, but in any case, where the mole is left to "moot" at will, these excrescences will soon show so thick over the ground as to render a considerable portion of the grass unavailable for pasturage; and if meadow land, for hay, there will not only be a shorter crop, but a more frequent sharpening of the scythe, causing extra trouble to the mowers. "Scattering" these heaps by spade, bush-harrow or chain-harrow is the usual remedy; which to be effectually applied needs now and then repeating. Some farmers, however, deem prevention better than cure; hence the calling of Mole-Catcher.

This individual is general, indeed almost universally, a man past the prime of life, and often aged; for mole-catching is an industry which tasks neither bodily strength nor activity. Still it has its requirements; these being familiarity with the animal's habits and the ways and means for capturing it. Dogs are not available for this purpose, nor digging; since neither dog nor digger can open the ground after a mole as fast as it can burrow before them. The gun or other weapon is equally useless for such a chase; moles rarely coming to the surface save during the night's darkness. One may live in a district where these animals abound almost for a lifetime and yet never see a live mole. Plenty of dead ones, true; but these have all been killed underground—in a trap. The mode of capture is as follows: *Talparius* seeing some "hills" that have been recently thrown up, the work of the preceding night, knows there is a subterranean tunnel between them, the "run." Choosing one of the freshest, he brushes aside the loose earth, to find a hole underneath; the orifice of a vertical shaft through which the mould has been cast up. This communicates with the horizontal gallery some two or three inches below the surface; the orifice itself, which is circular, being scarce two inches in diameter. Enlarging it a little, the mole-catcher inserts his trap; an article of iron-ware, with double-grippers on hinges like a pair of nut-crackers, and worked by a steel spring. When set, a thin plate of iron holds them apart, this being places vertically to close up the horizontal passage like a door. Then all is carefully covered over with the earth, so as to exclude the light; for if the mole sees light—and these animals see perfectly, notwithstanding the notion of their being blind—it knows things are not as it left them, and will shy the trap, even coming out upon the surface, and so passing it. If unsuspicious, however, in its ramblings along the "run," it will jab its snout against the obstructing plate, spring the trigger, and get caught between the grippers, losing its life on the instant.

For the sake of cheapness, the traps are made of common cast-iron, all save the springs; since the professional mole-catcher needs a goodly number of them. The price is six-pence each, though in past times they cost much more, and then *Talparius* employed a wooden trap of his own construction, the well-known sort having for spring power the rebound of a bent sapling. Some of these are still in use; and it is no uncommon sight while passing along the roads to see in field or meadow adjacent the little slate-colored quadruped hoisted high in air and swinging at the extremity of a bow-like rod.

There is still another mode of taking Talpa—the box-trap, which is a square or oblong box sunk into the earth, across the run, the ground having been hollowed out for it. A piece of board arranged on balance hinges inside the box, and on a level with the bottom of the run, carries the passage over as by a bridge. Rather should I say, seems to do so; for when the mole, attempting it, reaches a certain point, its weight sends the swing bridge down, and it is itself precipitated to the bottom of the box, out of which it cannot climb. This elaborate structure is only used in the "main runs"—not those temporarily traversed in pursuit of worms—where many moles are expected to come along and tumble into it. And often many do; the box sometimes, when left long unvisited, being found nearly full. Generally, too, most of them are dead, and partially eaten up; those that survive having been guilty of cannibalism! For the mole, apparently a gentle, innocent creature, is the very reverse; fierce as tiger and voracious as wolf or hyena. Partly for this reason the box-trap is only occasionally used, and then rather clandestinely; there being a sentiment against it on the score of cruelty.

I need not say the professional Mole-Catcher traps the mole neither for the sport of the thing nor on his own account. There would be no profit thereby; since no use whatever is made of the trapped animals. Even the skins, than which there are few others affording a prettier fur, or better for warmth, are thoughtlessly thrown away; only now and then some individual of peculiar tastes being seen wearing a waistcoat of them. *Talparius*, however, unless specially employed to collect and preserve them, invariably lets them go to naught, or rather bands all over, body, bones and skin, to those for whom he has done the trapping. They are his bounty warrants, and their ultimate destination is to swing on the branches of a tree, or get nailed up against the gable-end of a barn, in companionship with crows, magpies and other "vermin." The Mole-Catcher's work is done by special contract, his engagement being with farmers, country gentlemen and others occupying land.

THE MOLE-CATCHER AND THE RAT-CATCHER

His scale of remuneration in most parts of the country is threepence per head; but if a "garden mole" he charges double. There is no difference in the species of the animal; a "garden mole" being simply one that has taken to haunting in the kitchen or flower garden, where from the nature of the ground it is more difficult to coax them into a trap. This at least is the Mole-Catcher's alleged reason for demanding double pay. On farms where moles are not so plenteous as to be a pest, and ever non some where they are, the services of the professional *Talparius* are dispensed with, the farmer either doing the work of extermination for himself, or having it done by one of his ordinary laborers. There is little skill required; only setting the traps, and seeing to their being cleared and reset whenever a capture has been made. Moles are caught at all times of the year; though mostly in winter. But the real harvest of the professional Mole-Catcher is in March—the rutting season of the animals. Then he sets his traps on the main or permanent runs, along with the males, in pursuit of the females, or battling between themselves, are constantly going and coming; and so are quickly and easily caught.

Another of England's odd rural industries, which gives occasional employment to a few, is that of The Rat-Catcher. It might be supposed that he and the Mole-Catcher would be one and the same individual. But it is not so, or very rarely; the men as a rule holding existences and leading different sorts of life; in short, differing in character, ways and habits as much as in their *métiers*, or more. As already said, the Mole-Catcher is usually of mature age, and I may add, though not as a consequence, also of subdued, sober demeanor; while the professional killer of rats is a keeper and owner of ferrets, which he occasionally employs in rabbiting on his own account, though not on his own land—in short, is a bit of a poacher. Leaving his poaching to one side, however, his legitimate business is, as with the Mole-Catcher, a matter of contract. Where a farmstead or other premises chances to be infested with rats, he gets an engagement to clear them out, and comes, bringing his ferrets along with him. These, trained to the work, soon effect the clearance, entering every hole and cranny in barn, stable, granary or rick-yard, driving out the ugly rodents to be caught and killed by dogs, or trampled to death under the thick-soled, hob-nailed shoes of the attendant farm hands.

The tariff of the Rat-Catcher is exactly the same as that quoted for mole-trapping—threepence per head, or tail. And as if to make the parallelism symmetrically complete, for a rat killed inside the dwelling-house, as with a mole in the garden, the charge is double! The annual amount of emolument accruing to the men of either calling is of course variable and dependent on circumstances, such as the frequency or infrequency of their engagements, and the plenteousness or scarcity of the "game." For the time occupied at it, however, the job is generally remunerative; and I have known of a *Talparius* claiming payment for a score of moles trapped within the twenty-four houses; and a rat-catcher the same for three dozen dead rats, killed by his ferrets in the course of a single forenoon.

VIII.
Bark Strippers, Hurdle-Makers and Charcoal Burners.

Original publication date: May 14, 1882.

If I mistake not, most Americans are under the impression that in England there is nothing, or not much, in the way of woods. This is an erroneous idea, however, as in many districts there are large tracts of woodland, and in nearly all more or less of them. I do not speak of the half score great "forests" of Government belonging; not of woods owned by private individuals, the territorial magistrates of the land; usually the surroundings of their grand country mansions. In mountainous and hilly districts they are often of considerable extent, covering square miles, and mostly occupying declivities too steep to be conveniently arable. But there are also many tracts of woodland on level ground, where the soil is too poor to be worth tilling; and sometimes where worth it, such are maintained by plutocrats regardless of the cost, partly for the "grandeur" of the thing, but as much to make covers for game. True, only inside the park or in the immediate vicinity of the mansion are the trees permitted to attain any great age or size; the outside timber being converted into money as soon as it becomes available for certain economic purposes, and therefore salable. This occurs periodically, at intervals of from twenty to twenty-five years; as it has been found that such young trees pay better than older ones, the uses to which they are put being to make wheel-spokes, laths, hurdles, field gates for farms, and the like. The bark, too, is a valuable commodity disposable at the tanyards, as is also the charcoal obtained from the "lop and top" a requisite in many ironworks. Hence the industries of Bark-Stripping, Hurdle-Making and Charcoal Burning.

In a woodland tract of large extent this work of utilization is almost continuously going on; for although the trees are not available till after twenty years' growth, the fallage is not all done at the same time, but extends over many years, in each of which a section of the wood is doomed. It is not altogether deforested, however; the young saplings being left to stand and grow up to trees in their turn, so that while one portion of the timber is being cut down others are getting ready for the axe in various stages of advancement.

It is The Bark-Stripper who leads off; his work commencing about the middle of April, when the sap begins to flow; for without this his task would be difficult or scarcely practicable. He has three spells at it, as in England there are three separate "runnings" of the sap in trees. The first, or spring sap as called, continued for a period four or five weeks, when it ceases to flow. After a brief interval it commences running again but only for a short while, till stagnancy once more ensues. This is also of short continuance, and is succeeded by the last, or "midsummer sap," in late June the earlier days of July; after which the business of bark-stripping is at an end for the year. A dangerous business it is while it lasts; though likely the reader of this will wonder at my saying so. For, I take it, your strippers in the States do their work with the trees felled and lying along the ground. Sometimes it is so in England, where the timber is large and intended for house-building, props in mines, railway sleepers and such like. But the small sort, meant for the other purposes I have spoken of, calls for a different manipulation; and would be spoiled, or at least rendered less fit for its uses, were the trees cut down before being barked. The stripping, there, is done on the tree as it stands, the cutting down to come afterward; hence the danger.

The mode of procedure is as follows: The stripper first makes him a rough ladder, by which he may ascend the tree's trunk as far as it will reach. IF above that there still be a portion of the bole without branches to give him foothold, he drives in a series or iron pins, made expressly for this purpose, and by these continues his climb from one to the other. On getting to the highest ascendable point of the trunk, he wriggles himself out upon the branches as far as these will bear him; then peels off their bark, and lets it fall to the earth. The tool employed in the "stripper"—a little iron blade, steel-tipped, and in shape resembling the ace of spades, with a wooden handle in socket; the whole implement being about the size and weight of a mortising chisel. But for stripping the trunk, where the bark is thicker and more adherent, he uses a "stripper" of somewhat bigger blade and longer shaft, though otherwise the same. Dealing with the larger limbs, he "chips" them—that is, notches them circumferentially—at distances of about three feet apart; then making a longitudinal incision, he enters the stripper and "heaves" the bark off in sections. His work is begun on the topmost branches of the tree and carried downward; for it done the other way, the already peeled and slippery limbs would make it both more difficult and more dangerous. When all the boughs have been decorticated the truck is attacked,, it too being "chipped" into sections and stripped from above downward. If of large circumference, the iron steps are driven in at distances all around it, for then the tick, heavy bark calls for extra strength and firm support in the "heaving off," the stripper using his arms, head and shoulders to detach it.

 The danger lies chiefly in barking the upper branches; and it is a real danger, oft ending in death. No year passes without record of more than one stripper—in some years many of them—receiving sore injury or being killed outright by falling from the trees. Passing a wood where they have been at work, and seeing the branches bare almost to their topmost twigs, one can well believe this; wondering, too, at their having ventured out so far. True, they are not necessitated to take such risk, it being understood that where the branch is deemed untrustworthy they may hack it off and do the barking on the ground. But these fellows are very fearless, and too often very reckless.

The reader will be wanting to know what is the reward for this perilous work; toilsome work too, as anyone will know who has ever climbed a tree. Indeed, when his day's task is done the stripper may be oft seen returning to this home in hobbling gait, thoroughly used up. But his wage—what is it? Well, that depends on how he may have succeeded at his work, as the payment is pro rata—by the ton of bark. The price per ton, not for the bark but the stripping it, is different for different sized timber. Where the trees are large it is less and with what is called "coppice wood" more; not that the latter is more difficult to strip, but form its taking longer time to get the same quantity off it. The scale ranges from £1 up to £1 10s, per ton, but the average rate will be about $5. This includes "railing" the bark; that is resting it on end against rails supported on forked uprights, in order that it may get dry. He is a clever stripper who can make one ton in the week, working twelve hours a day; and the ordinary hands fall far short of that, some not exceeding half a ton. From this the rate of wages may be deduced.

The strippers work in "gangs" of eight or ten—and are employed and paid by the "ganger," he being a man who has undertaken the whole job, dealing directly with the owner of the timber. With each of the smaller gangs there is a woman whose business it is to "rail" the bark, and a boy who carries it to her; the larger gangs employing two railers and two carriers. Nor are the trees stripped her and there irregularly, but taken in "breadths" or sections, of sixty yards wide, running longitudinally through the wood. The sixty yards width has reference to the after convenience of carrying the "cordwood" when the timber is cut down, which is stacked or "corded" along a central line, and so thirty years from either edge of the section. With this, however, the stripper has nothing to do, his *métier* being at an end when the bark is all off and railed. There are after processes in preparing it for the tanyard, but these are carried on far away from the wood, in the barkyard of the dealer, and mostly by women.

It is not necessary here to enter upon a description of the

felling of the timber, a work about which there is nothing peculiar. It is done by woodmen accustomed to handle an axe and among them are many of the strippers, now released from their own idiosyncrasy of trade. It gives them a few days' employment; and when that is over, they look out for other jobs, some of them taking to mines, if these be near, others to farm work. Still the wood is not deserted; there remaining in it men of at least two other trades— The Hurdle-Maker and the Charker. I do not know whether hurdle-making be an American industry; and therefore what I am about to say of it may be telling a well-known tale. Still it is a calling which needs but brief description, and with that though I shall venture to give a slight account of it. In England the *raison d'etre* of the hurdle is chiefly the keeping of sheep. Throughout most of the winter these animals are removed from the pasture lands and put into fields of growing turnips, or "Swedes," on which they need "penning"; for if left to ramble about at will they would destroy as many, or more, of the roots than they might eat. To avoid this the hurdle is called into requisition, and with these they are inclosed in "pen," taking the field in sections successively; the shifting being done by the shepherd, as the roots, in each become exhausted. Of hurdles there are several kinds; "five-barred," high and strong enough to make fences for cattle; "four-barrel," for sheep; and the "wattle hurdle," which bears resemblance to rough basket-work. The first and last, however, are exceptional; and the four-barred or "sheep hurdle" is the one I now have to do with. It is six feet in length and four in height or breadth, exclusive of the pointed "spags," to be driven into the ground in setting it up. As its name implies, it has four horizontal bars, which are morticed into three uprights of stouter make, the material employed being usually oak, but sometimes chestnut or willow. A rough affair it is, neither saw nor plane being used in its construction, only the axe, chopper and draw-knife. The bars and uprights are obtained by splitting, or "ripping," in woodman's phraseology; and when cut to length and shape, knocked hastily together; a particular sort of nails, called "hurdle nails," being used to bind them.

The hurdle-maker does his work in the wood, if the weather be fine; but should it rain or snow, or the wind be chilly—for he works in winter as well as summer—he has a shed to shelter him, with a fire convenient. He returns to his home at night, however, though not to his meals, these being eaten and often cooked on the spot where he toils. Thee wooden hurdles sell for sixteen shillings the dozen, or about 30 cents each. Formerly they were dearer; but the reduced price of iron has brought a powerful competitor into the field; for though the iron hurdle costs three or four times as much, it is a better article and believed to be cheaper in the end. Still the other, from the less outlay at starting, holds a conspicuous place in the farming industry of England, and will doubtless continue to do so. It is by the dozen the hurdle-maker is paid for his work, the scale of payment being five shillings or fivepence each. And he will work dexterously and hard who puts together five hurdles in the day; or in other words earns 50 cents. Such is the reward for labor in rural England; skilled labor at that!

Of the three callings which form the subject of this letter, that of The Charcoal-Burner is the most exclusive as regards the men who follow it. They are few in numbers, but have rarely any other business, since charcoal-burning gives employment at all seasons of the year; and though apparently a simple thing, it is not so, calling for both knowledge and skill. The material they have to deal with the "lop and top" of the trees, or cordwood, and their modus operandi as follows: A floor or "pit" is prepared by clearing the rubbish off the ground, and then hollowing out a circular space some six or eight inches in depth, but of no fixed diameter; this being dependent on the quantity of wood to be "charked" in that particular pit lying conveniently near for carriage to it. In the centre of the floor four or five short, stoutish billets are placed with ends touching, so as themselves to inclose a circular space of a foot or eighteen inches diameter, and on these the ends of the charking sticks are rested slantingly and radiating like the spokes of a wheel.

On the outer rim of this first layer a second is placed in similar manner; and so, till the pile is complete when it shows the form of an obtuse cone, or hemisphere. Around the central axis, however, is a hollow space or chimney, which has been left open for the fire; and this first kindled at its bottom, by dropping down some burning faggots, in due time permeates the whole mass. But before any flames show on the surfaces the pile is carefully covered over with a stratum of sods, and so kept, not an airhole being left open. Were the wood allowed to blaze up, there would be no charcoal—only ashes. And just to prevent this is the "charker's" business—a

thing of the night as well as the day. It needs two men at least to undertake the task, who in turns sit up all night to watch the fires of the different pits—for there will be several on the burn at the same time—going the rounds from one to another, and patching with a fresh sod or shovelful of earth any spot where flames may threaten an outburst. In fine, when the fires burn themselves out the charcoal is a made thing, and only needs separating from the ashes and earthy matter which have got mixed with it from the superimposed sods.

The "charkers" are paid for their work by measure of the quantity of charcoal produced, the standard of measurement being a large oblong basket holding about three bushels. The exact amount of their earnings is not easily fixed, but certainly they do not make fortunes by "charking," any more than could by bark-stripping or the fabrication of hurdles. These men stay nearly all their time in the woods, never returning home, even at night, for weeks or months together. They dwell in huts erected by themselves—quaint affairs of conical form made of poles set sloping against one another, gathered in at the top, and thatched with a coating of turf, just as are their charking fires. Many of these huts are made large enough to hold half a dozen men; though rarely occupied by more than two or three; when there will be a like number of rude beds in them, with a full paraphernalia of cooking utensils. Some of the bachelor "charkers," who have not ambition to pay house rent, stick to these sylvan abodes throughout the year, whether they be at work or not.

IX.
The Gamekeeper.

Original publication date: May 28, 1882.

Not the least conspicuous figure in the tableau of English rural life, and almost a specialty of it, is The Gamekeeper. Though few in numbers, compared with the men of most other callings, gamekeepers are found all over the country; more or less of them in every shire, according to the number of gentry resident in it; for, with slight exceptions, only to the establishments of these is the gamekeeper an attachment. But to give intelligible account of him, his work and his ways, it will be necessary to enter upon the question of game-preserving in England, with the laws relating to it. And first as to the game itself.

The *feræ natura* of the British Isles that takes rank as "game," both the furred and the feathered, are few in species, the hare being the sole representative of the former, though until lately the rabbit had a place in the list. Deer (red, roe and fallow) are in a sense regarded as game; but as these exist in a semi-wild state in certain limited districts (chiefly in the Highlands and islands of Scotland), they do not come with the scope of this article. Neither do deer kept in parks; which may be accounted in the same category with sheep, cattle or other domesticated animals. The feathered games consists of the bustard, pheasant, partridge (gray and red-legged), quail, grouse (black, red and ptarmigan), woodcock, snipe (Jack, common, and solitary), and lastly the landrail. Not all of these are found in any one district of the country, at least in large numbers, and in many shires several of the species are altogether wanting. The bustard, though still figuring in the game statutes, has been long extinct in the British Isles; while the ptarmigan is only found in the north of Scotland. Grouse, too, red and black, are rare in

England save in its northern counties, their habitat being the moor and the mountain. They are plenteous, however, in Yorkshire and Cumberland, as also in some parts of Wales and Ireland; but, as with many others of the game birds, North Britain is the land of their abundance. Snipe and woodcock, too, as also quails, are of local distribution and semi-migratory; while the landrail, a true migrant species, is scarce considered by the sportsman or preserver of game.

In England the ownership of game, whatever its kind, is vested in the proprietor of the land, and not the occupier, unless by special understanding and agreement between the two. This is the universal theory and practice, supposed to have origin in ancient rights of forestry and domain. But why go so far back for an argument to support the privilege? For if it be not a right of property, I know not what is. Would space permit, I could easily prove this right of ownership in game, but taking it for granted, I proceed to speak of the statutes enacted for its preservation, generally known as the "Game Laws." In England these are not intended merely to save the game from destruction but to maintain its value as a food commodity, an actual money's worth, with an eye also to the "sport" in its capture. That the former motive had precedence in the making of the protector statues is evinced by the fact of all the birds and animals protected by them being those most esteemed as food delicacies, and so desirable property. Therefore "sport" along cannot be looked upon as the object of game-preserving; only a conjoint and lesser factor, with a keen sense of the more substantial only one underlying it. Whatever the *raison d'etre*, the Game Laws of Great Britain prohibit all landless people from killing or capturing game, unless with the leave of the landlord. But neither can these give permission, nor kill it themselves, without first obtaining a "game license" or "game certificate," as the statutes term it, for which the annual payment is £3. If not taken out till November 1, after there have been two months of shooting, and the "gilt gone off the gingerbread," then the price is £2. In either case the license terminates with the commencement of the close season, April 5, and has to be renewed for the next year. This "game certificate" has nothing to do with what is called a "gun license"—another of those petty machinations by which England's protective government exacts revenue while posing in the front rank of free trade; the amount of the mulet being ten shillings per annum, which gives no right to kill game, but only to own and carry a gun!

But to return to the special subject. For game-preserving, a gamekeeper is of course required; and nearly every gentleman owning landed property has one or more in his employ. If the estate be a large one, and the owner much addicted to sporting, there will be a "head keeper," "under keeper," and staff of "watchers"; these last being men under command of the keeper who perambulate the "covers," or look out after poachers and other trespassers. Their duties are chiefly nocturnal, though in part performed by day; and on the estates of wealthy grandees the tribe—keepers and watchers included—frequently foot up to fifteen or twenty individuals. Such princely establishments, however, are exceptional; and the usual gamekeeping staff is the keeper himself, with a watcher, or it may be a couple of such assistants. Nor is the aid given by these restricted to watching trespassers; they have often to render it in personal encounters with the latter—desperate fights where firearms are used on both sides—as the poachers do not always run away. This, however, is a matter requiring more detail than present space allows.

For dwelling place the gamekeeper is provided with a neat, comfortable cottage known as the "keeper's lodge," picturesquely situated, nearly always in the midst of woods and far away from other houses; this for the convenience of his being at all times near the area of operations. Around it there will be an acre or two of cleared ground—not garden, but grass-ground, on which appears an array of little box-like houses with pitched roofs. These are the "kennels" or dog-boxes, and there are dogs chained to them of several breeds, but all of sporting specialty—pointers, setters, water-spaniels and retrievers. Other wooden structures at some distance apart are the "cubs" and coops, where young pheasants are hatched and brought up by common barnyard fowls before being turned out into the covers. It is the keeper's great ambition, as that of his master, to show a pheasant preserve well stocked with these birds when October 1 comes around and friends are invited to take part in the battue. For attainment of this pheasants' eggs are an article of barter and sale, and readily sell for a shilling each, the purchasers being the men themselves, and the only ones, supposed to own pheasants. The traffic is carried on rather surreptitiously, since it is well known that most of these eggs must have come out of other preserves—it may be those of a near neighbor—and stolen. Still the trade goes on, the keeper managing the delicate negotiation, about which he "keeps dark," while his master winks at it. For such and other like reasons, it is a common thing to hear said that many gentlemen's pheasants "cost them a guinea a head" before a single bird has been shot. This sounds big, proclaiming the owner a man of unlimited means and open hand, regardless of the expense and caring only for the sport. The assertion has long gone unchallenged; yet it is anything but true. There may be occasional instances of plutocrats—and among them, more than any, the *nouveaux riches*—who squander in this silly way; but to my knowledge most game preserves, gentry or otherwise, are game dealers as well, with a keen eye to business, and every pheasant, hare or partridge killed, save what they keep for their own tables, is packed and sent off for sale to the cities. And it is an economy that pays them well; in most cases, if I mistake not, returning the expense of preserving—keepers, watchers and everything—with some profit besides.

    A notable feature which distinguishes the game-keeper's dwelling from that of the ordinary cottager is its gable end. Against this will be seen nailed up the skins of all sorts of animals, to him known as "vermin" —weasels, stoats, polecats, and possibly that of the badger; though the fox, more destructive to game than any, will not be there. The killing of Reynard would be deemed a "dirty trick" on the part of a country gentleman, and in most cases the keeper's master is himself a fox-hunter. In this, "gamekeeper's museum," as it is jocularly styled, the predatory birds hold a conspicuous place—all the species of hawks, with the raven, carrion crow, magpie and jay; even the rook and jackdaw figuring there as suspected suckers of eggs. A plentitude of such specimens gives proof of the keeper's zeal and industry in the performance of his duties.

These duties vary according to the time of year. In spring, when the shooting season is over, and early summer, his ordinary work is to look after the breeding of the game-birds, note their places of nesting, and see that they are not disturbed or interfered with. Then, too, is his time of best activity for the extirpation of "vermin"; all sorts of it being at this season tamer and so easier to circumvent. The bird-nesting boy, also, needs looking after, the damage done by him being often as great or greater than that accruing from the regular poacher. As autumn approaches, the keeper finds full occupation in the training of young dogs to the gun; and it may be giving some young master his first lessons in *venerie*. Later on, when the shooting recommences, on all shooting days he is the *compagnon de chasse* of his employer and such friends as the latter may invite to shoot with him, the keeper having an eye to their sporting tackle, to see that it is in proper condition, and otherwise lending them a hand. This period of the year, with its special *métier*, is his merriest, as also most lucrative, since he receives many a handsome "tip" from the strangers to whom it is his care to be civil.

The regular wages of a gamekeeper, reckoned by the week, vary according to circumstances. If "head keeper" on a large estate, with first-class character and qualifications, his pay will be high in proportion. But the average for ordinary keepers is about £1 per week, exclusive of his lodge, which he holds rent free. There are also other advantages obtainable by him, as perquisites received for the breaking in of dogs belonging to his master's friends, and a percentage on the sale of rabbits; with occasionally some sold the master wots not of. Sometimes, also, the keeper's wife follows an economy which adds to their common income; having an engagement to raise and provide the table of the mansion with eggs, poultry, capons, and such commodities, often on a grand scale. From all this it will be seen that gamekeepers are better off than the men of their class who follow most other industries in England. Few of them there are, when sober and saving, that in old age have not put aside sufficient to live upon comfortably if not luxuriously. But before this period arrives there are also few who have not passed through scenes of trial and danger, rarely to come out of them unscathed, and often escaping death as it were by "the skin of their teeth." In truth a perilous life is that of the English gamekeeper; all by reason of him next in order for delineation—The Poacher.

X.
The Poacher

Original publication date: June 4, 1882

There is no parish in England without its Poacher, and in some two, three, or more may be found. I do not speak of occasional transgressors of the Game Laws, as idle fellows out upon Sundays or holidays, who spend them in the capture of game partly for the pot, but as much by way of pastime. These are poachers too, punishable and punished all the same; but they are not accounted in the category of the regular, or as he is often styled, "professional," poacher. True, he does not style himself so, only by his deeds having earned the designation; instead he generally pretends to have some trade or other industry, and ostensibly practises it during the day. When night comes on, down go his trade tools, and in their place arming himself with nets, wire-snares,, gins and gun, he is off to the game preserves. But there is also the poacher *pur sang*, who disdains all such subterfuge, regardless of reputation as of law, who for his livelihood depends solely on the sale of the game he may capture. Not such a poor dependence is it either; considering that hares sell for over a dollar each, pheasants the same, partridges a dollar and a half the brace, and woodcocks two dollars the couple. True, these are the retail prices; but the licensed game-dealer himself—he must be licensed—has to give figures close up to them, whether he purchases from the owners of preserves or otherwise. He is not supposed to negotiate with the poacher at all, though he often undoubtedly does, and as the traffic is illegal, with as much danger to the buyer as the seller, the reduction in price is not so great as might be supposed. In any case, the poacher receives a fair remuneration; and the more when his dealings are direct with the consumer, as they generally are. He can always dispose of hare or pheasant, *sub rosa*, to the semi-gentility residing in villas, and the shopkeepers of the towns; besides there is never wanting in any neighborhood a publican who makes surreptitious game-dealing a specialty, and is ready to act as his "fence" and receiver. It will thus be seen that he has no difficulty in finding a market for his commodities; and, supposing him to take only a single hare or pheasant in the night, greater are his gains than those of the poor laborer who toils all day for a scant two-shilling wage. From a night's poaching, however, there will frequently accrue many heads of game; hence the temptation to follow it as a profession.

In the pursuit of this unlawful calling, the regular poacher displays remarkable skill; having an intimate acquaintance with all the ways of the game birds and animals, and the modes of capturing them. He will the find the tree on which pheasants roost at night by the accumulation of their droppings underneath; the hare he catches in wire snares set in the breaks or "grats" of hedges, where "puss" is in the habit of passing through; while the partridge he takes in the stubble, by means of long nets; a confrere or two assisting him to extend them. Sometimes a whole covey will be thus captured at a single draw. Passing through a district of country where game is zealously preserved, one often sees a stubble-field with branches of hawthorn sticking up here and there over it; the object being to obstruct night-netting by poachers. True, these might pluck the thorns up and clear them out of their way; but in doing so the birds would be flushed and cleared off also. In most neighborhoods, the rabbit is the poacher's best source of supply and emolument; its capture paying him better than even that the nobler sours of game. And of late more than ever; the price of rabbits having risen in a remarkable degree. But a few years ago, the indigenous wild species could have been purchased in any part of England for sixpence or 12 cents; now it is three times as much. This is partly due to the increased scale of prices for butcher's meat, the use of rabbits' flesh being found an economy.

But there is also a greater appreciation of it in modern days as a delicacy, many people esteeming it so, and when properly cooked it is. Of course the poacher does not get eighteen-pence for a rabbit; but he has no difficulty in obtaining a tenpence or a shilling. He had needs, however, be cautious in his dealings with this as with other game, and so also they who buy from him; for although rabbits are not strictly regarded as game, they are equally under protection of the Game Statutes as property. A recent Act has somewhat relaxed the law relating to them, as also to hares, giving tenant farmers a limited leave to kill them on their own land. Agricultural depression, with the outcry raised at the damage done to crops by the "ground game," as these are called, led to the passing of this Act; which, however, has no beneficial bearing on the poor man, against whom game and sport are alike tabooed. As to the poacher, it affects him for the worse; making every farmer a zealous watcher and aid to the gamekeeper; still poaching is not put down, but goes on as ever.

A gang of three or four poachers, working together, will capture two or three score rabbits in a night's excursion. They take them in various ways; one of which is by wire snares, set as for hares in the hedge-brakes or on the beaten "runs," when the rabbits are abroad feeding; then the poacher's dog, trained to do his part, chases the animals into them. Sometimes the snares are left set over day, to be revisited on the following night; but this is rather risky, leaving traces that may discovered and utilized by the keeper and his watchers. When the warren itself is attached, the poacher goes about his work in a different way, calling the ferret to his aid. The mode of procedure is to fix nets over the mouths of the burrows, then send the ferrets in, when the rabbits bolting out are enmeshed and get their necks instantly broken by a wrench from the poacher's wrist. There is no poacher without a pair or more of these tame and trained weasels, his most efficient assistants; and for a reason—imparted to me in confidence by one of the fraternity—the white, pink eyed variety is preferred to the brown or "fitchet ferret"; the former from its color being easier seen in the darkness and so better for poaching, mostly done at night. In addition to his ferrets the poacher keeps a dog, and sometimes tow, in which case one will be a half-bred greyhound or lurcher for "coursing" hares, when the opportunity offers at early morn or on a moonlight night. He carries a gun, too, though not always; and even thus armed used it sparingly, dreading betrayal by its report. The gun itself is peculiar and known as a "poacher's gun," being short-barrelled and easily taken to pieces for deposit in the inside pocket of his coast. These are ample, in fact the who skirt is a pocket round and round, capable of containing quite a hamperful of hares and pheasants.

In the personal appearance of the out-and-out poacher, there is an idiosyncrasy, both as to dress and general bearing. His garb is very much like that of a gamekeeper, only not so neat nor new, and would better compared with a suit the gamekeeper has cast off. The coast is of a brown but faded velveteen with four outside flap pockets besides the great inner one; vest of the same material; knee-breeches and gaiters of fustian or corduroy; and stout, heavy-soled half-boots, hobnailed and laced. Add a soft felt hat worn slouchingly, with a neckerchief loosely knotted, usually a red cotton kerchief, and you have the English poacher in the costume he most commonly affects. Not less characteristic is the expression of his features, which, though they may not be naturally sinister, still have a cast about them telling of prison experience. No wonder they should; for rare is the poacher who has not spent a portion of his life inside the walls of a jail and been locked up repeatedly for spells longer or shorter. An outlaw by his own seeking and bringing about, he is often deserving of outlawry in its worst form—a very wretch and ruffian. But it would be untruthful to say that all poachers are so, or even the majority of them. Many show traits of character more commendable than condemnable; among these a proud independence of spirit, which possibly has much to do in making them what they are. For it cannot be denied that in the mind of the English poor man there is an instinctive idea of resistance to laws seeming oppressive—no more can it be questioned his too oft having reason for it. One good quality the poacher possesses in a high degree—courage; and the very fact of his being a poacher is proof of it. But there is other and better evidence, though bad for him, produced at almost every Petty Sessions, and certainly at every Assizes; often proof of too much courage, getting him sentenced to penal servitude for life, if not actually sent to the scaffold. "Affrays," as they are termed, between parties of poachers and gamekeepers are of frequent occurrence; fierce encounters, with firearms used on both sides, as in a battle, often resulting in fatal wounds or death itself upon the spot. When bent upon such desperate resistance the poachers generally go disguised and with masked or blackened faces, though not always.

The penalty for poaching varies with the nature of the offence; the season of the year, the hours of the day or night, even religion affecting it. As for instance, taking game on a Sunday or Christmas Day subjects the taker to a fine of £5, and for killing game birds during the *close* season the fine is £1 per head of those killed. These penalties, however, are not special to poachers, the owners of the game itself being liable to them. The laws that more affect the poacher come under the heading of "Trespass," and he is termed a "trespasser in pursuit of game." When caught so trespassing in the day (which is defined as "from the beginning of the last hour before sunrise and concluding with the expiration of the first hour after sunset") the penalty is £3 and costs. If the trespass be by night it is punished not by fine but imprisonment, and the term is accumulative; for a first offence three months with sureties required at its expiration; for a second, six months, with double the amount in money securities, not to offend again; and in case of a third or further trespass it is treated as "misdemeanor." And if the trespasser refuse giving his name to those who have the right to demand it of him, offer resistance to them, or use violence, the punishment assumes a still more serious phase, especially if he be a known poacher; and above all, where there are several acting together and armed.

Catching a poacher; from *The Graphic*, October 17, 1874.

As may be supposed, gamekeepers and policemen are empowered to make summary arrest of those they may suspect of being poachers, and were this power confined to its legitimate purpose there would be no great harm in it. Unfortunately, however, it is not thus restricted, but too often stretched and abused, especially by the policeman. Exulting in the possession of this almost irresponsible authority, he also glories in making a display of it; the consequence being that many a poor laborer returning wearied from his day's work, with no more thought of game-stealing than the man in the moon, is brought up by hail as of highwayman to "stand and deliver." Then to have his coat or "slop" pockets searched, the "pail," too, in which he has carried his meagre provisions to the field, to see if he be not carrying home hare, rabbit, pheasant or partridge. All this on a public road, an ordinary occurrence too, and in that rural England which, as I see by an editorial in THE TRIBUNE, an American writer—Mr. Winter—has depicted as "almost beyond parallel peaceful, gentle and beautiful." Beautiful it may be, and in many parts certainly is, with, as this writer further says, "rural regions thoroughly cultivated and exquisitely adorned." But for the "peaceful" and "gentle" Mr. Winter will have to go elsewhere; unless by gentleness he means abject submissive meekness and his peace be that of the workhouse, the jail and the grave. To the poor man of England there is no peace, but ever war—constant toil with attendant trouble, to end only with his life. And I have no hesitation in affirming that there are few such men whose lives are not shortened by the struggle—aye, many of them by years. Could this writer only look into the cottages of these poor men, as I do daily, and witness their early decrepitude through diseases consequent on exposure to weather, with overwork and often stinted food, he would not there find his "potential, manifold and abundant sources of beauty, refinement and peace." And were he out for a nocturnal stroll along one of England's country roads, with a threadbare coat upon his back, to be stopped by the rural policeman and have his pockets turned inside out,—no rare nor problematical occurrence,—it would doubtless modify his ideas about the poetry of English rural life, making very plain unpleasant prose of it.

From *The Illustrated London News,* July 4, 1846.

XI.
County Society

Original publication date: June 11, 1882

In England "County Society" is a phrase of high sounding significance, and to belong to it an object of mighty ambition, those who do being considered the *crème de la crème*. I believe there is no other country where so many of the higher classes have their homes "in the country"; far more than the majority residing in it permanently all the year round, with the exception of a week or two during what is called the "London season." The reasons for this are various. Besides the inclinings to rural life and scenery common to all, a passion for field sports is innate with Englishmen, and ever has been;—hence the preserving of game for the gun, all over the land, with foxes for hunting. Good roads also contribute to the delights of country life; making it not only pleasant to drive out, but convenient to dine out; from the ease of getting briskly whirled home, though the distance be ten or a dozen miles. As a result there are fine country houses in all the shires, many of them grand mansions, that will accommodate a numerous array of guests, and are rarely without some under their roofs. The English rural life need never be dull or lonely, and never is so to those who have the means of entertaining; instead cheerful, and often stirring and eventful as that of the town. In point of fact, only a very small proportion of England's gentry dwell continuously in town; they who have town houses having country ones as well, to which they retire when the fashionable season comes to a close. By "town" I of course mean the metropolis, London; for gentry, residing in the provincial towns or cities, as Manchester, Liverpool and the like, were an anomaly. Rich men reside there, or in their suburbs; having big houses, too, of the villa order, and maintaining style, with carriages and servants in livery. But these are not "gentry" according to the English idea; much less belong they to County Society.

To the chief elements composing County Society I have already alluded, when speaking of county organization; but it may be well to recapitulate them in fuller detail. They are the landed aristocracy, titled or untitled, with many who have little or no land, their kindred by marriage or otherwise; the clergy of the State Church; retired officers of the Army and Navy; "nabobs" returned from India, who have there amassed large fortunes, and whose origin, perhaps of the humblest, is unknown or forgotten; also men who have figured in the higher ranks of the Civil and Diplomatic services. But as the English Government jealously reserves the last-named service for the *filii nobiles* of the land, they would be in county society without it. All judges are in it, of course, with many barristers, most of these by right of birth, and some from having attained eminence in their profession or made money by it. Attorneys and solicitors, as they are somewhat promiscuously styled, have no claim or footing in county society; though many work their way into its edge, get admitted to its innermost circles, all its doors flying open to them as by magic at the touch of a golden key. The doctor enters it only exceptionally; and so the merchant and manufacturer,—save when very wealthy,—while farmers and all men engaged in ordinary trades or callings, with Nonconformist ministers, are rigorously excluded.

Its component materials being thus restricted, it will be easily understood that county society is not individually numerous, though in this respect there is a difference in the different shires; some having a greater number of resident gentry than others; and some even where these are almost non-existent. In an average county there will be 200 or 250 of them—I mean families. And now I am going to make an affirmation which will possibly cause surprise to most Americans, and anger to many Englishmen; that beyond those 250 families, less or more, there is not an inhabitant of any English county, or town either, who is a citizen as you understand citizenship in America; the gentry alone being invested with full civic rights. For they alone are eligible to all offices of honor and emolument, or at least to the attainment of them without effort, and almost as a matter of course. When any high office is attained by one of the common people, it is with a struggle and a strain, and its accomplishment a thing of gratulation and triumph. So, I repeat, that *in England there is no citizen, in the true sense of the word, save those who belong to her aristocracy.* I know the burst of indignation with which my assertion will be received, and how I shall get reviled for making it. But it is nevertheless true; and I am prepared with the substantiating proofs, regardless of those it may irritate.

Returning to the more immediate subject of my article, I need hardly say that county society affects grand airs, and looks down on all beneath it—which means almost everybody—with a proud, patronizing glance. No absolutely disdainful or supercilious is it; instead rather courteous and conciliatory, as it can well afford. Seated in its elegant equipage, with liveried servant on box and rumble, it has no fear of the *hoi polloi* being rude or over-familiar. And never are they, but often too much the reverse, addressing it hand in hand.

With such high privileges and assumptions, it would naturally be supposed that this charmed circle is exclusive to the extremest degree. And in a certain way so is it; personal worth, manhood, intellectuality, learning, culture of whatever kind, having no chance to enter or figure in it for their own sake. Yet I doubt if there by any other aristocracy in the world whose crust is more easily broken through by one armed with proper weapon—which is wealth. Plutus can at any time pierce it with his gold-tipped spear; send this crashing through it, as a bullet through an egg shell. And without any relation to character, or any other qualification Plutus may possess. He may be fool or knave, or both combined; it matters not, or not much, so long as he carry with him the necessary credential—money—the never-failing "open sesame" of county society's doors. How much does it take to open them? my American reader may inquire; from what I have said, possibly imagining them easy on the hinge and accessible to anyone wealthy enough to live without work, and keep a carriage, with two or three servants in livery. Nothing of the sort, however; the requirements for *entrée* into county society go beyond all that. He who climbs up to it on the money ladder must have enough to purchase a landed estate, with park and mansion, also some rentable farms whose tenants will be entitled to vote for the county member of Parliament. Having all this and settling down to county life, he will soon be "called upon" by the neighboring gentry; the sooner if he have a graceful wife, and two or three good-looking daughters—these wonderfully facilitating introduction to county society.

The amount of money required to effect this will not be the same in all the shires, but depend much on whether the resident families be themselves rich and grand magnates. Where many of these reside, introduction is more difficult, and Plutus needs to make a greater effort to obtain it. But in remote counties, where the gentry are comparatively poor—as they often are—there is less aversion to having him at their tables; indeed, they rather seek his company than disdain it. And if he be a very wealthy Plutus, he is not long in getting into high position and in turn patronizing them. I could mention several counties in which this practice is now prevailing; the ancient aristocracy being almost extinct, or having "taken a back seat"; their estates disentailed, and passed into the hands of the *nouveaux riches*, who occupy their old mansions. These newcomers into country society generally play the *grand riegneur* in princely style, giving sumptuous entertainments, many of them becoming masters of fox-hounds and affecting the old fox-hunting squire, with all his bluff bravoism and swagger. They also contribute largely to charities of the showy kind, especially those of the Church; for if Dissenters as tradesmen, they generally turn

Episcopalians [Anglicans] as squires, this being the fashionable religion. Holding the dispossessed squire's property they of course also occupy his pew in church, and many the grand organs, sets of bells, stained glass windows and other church decorations or restorations that are due to their munificence. "In fact," remarked an old rector to me the other day, with a jocose, cunning twinkle in his eye, "they are our best cows to give milk."

In saying that character has little or nothing to do with introduction to county society, and money much, if not all, I speak from facts that have come under my own observation and experience. Scores of instances I could adduce in proof of my statement, but one will suffice; and I affirm it to be a fair sample, while neither a rare or solitary one. Sometime ago, being the guest of Lady G——, the sister of a Duke, at a ball given in her country house, her husband, conversing with me, asked:

"Do you know Mr. L——? You see him yonder"; and he pointed to a gentleman on the opposite side of the room.

"Only by name and sight," I answered, recognizing the individual alluded to, whom I knew to be a rich man lately come to reside in the neighborhood, having purchased an estate with park, mansion and all the adjuncts.

"Did you ever hear how he came by his money—I mean made his first beginning?" was the next interrogatory volunteered by my host.

"I've heard some hints about it.:

"Well; I can tell you the whole story. In early life he kept a little drapery shop in one of the second-rate streets of London, replenishing his stock chiefly from what they call 'job lots,' which he bought for cash, without asking any questions as to where they came from. He had got a name for that sort of thing, and one day made a grand speculation by it, on Irish goods, The man who sold them to him had a large credit with the manufacturer and had never paid for them, in—tending to turn bankrupt—as soon after he did—he made them over to L—— for less than half their value, glad to get what he could for them. At this examination afterward, in the Court of Bankruptcy, it was made out a fraudulent transaction, and the Commissioner said Mr. L—— deserved to be standing on his trial as much as the bankrupt. Somehow or other L—— managed to get clear; and—look at him at him now!"

I did not need to look at him, neither to be told the tale, which was already known to me and notorious everywhere. Yet there was the ex-dealer in "job lots" figuring in best society, on an equal footing with it, his wife, sons and daughters too! All this in the house and at a ball given by a titled lady, one of the proudest of England's aristocracy!

At that same ball, and shortly after, my host further said to me: "You see that lady—her with such a load of jewelry on." He pointed to a fine-looking woman, who moved about sparkling like a glacier or stalactite under the lamps. On my nodding an affirmative he added: "That's Mrs. C——. Just look at her diamonds! I'm told she has full £20,000 worth of them in that tiara."

And Mrs. C—— was the wife of a London stockbroker, whose dealings were said to be anything but reputable! Who, then, will say that English aristocratic society is either strait-laced or exclusive?

XII.
County Society in Summer.

Original publication date: June 18, 1882.

It may interest the American reader to know how English "County Society" employs itself. Perhaps I should rather say enjoys itself, since this more concerns it than any serious occupation of life. Of course the gentlemen, heads of families, give some attention to business affairs, as affecting their estates; while wives and grown-up daughters devote a portion of their time to works of charity and mercy. I think I may say that a large minority of them do this; especially "in districts where looking after the poor in a sort of patronizing way is a thing of rivalry and fashion. Still, with the majority pleasure takes precedence of everything else; and from year's end to year's end it is with them a round of amusements, which vary with the seasons. Those incidental to summer do not commence until about the middle of the year, as during the spring and early summer months, the leaders of County Society are "in town," where it is itself supposed to be. For then is the "London season" —Parliament in session, theatres, operas, picture exhibitions, flower shows, Court receptions and drawing-rooms, with all the other frivolities, are in full swing. To take part in, or be present at, these is esteemed the correct thing; and not doing or being so were to be out of the fashion. They terminate at no exact date, as the London season is, more or less, caused by and coexistent with the sitting of Parliament, which by a perverse anachronism, retains England's aristocracy in town at the time country life is most enjoyable. It is generally over by the latter end of July, when rural life is resumed, with the sports and pastimes appertaining to it.

Formerly croquet was the great summer game and "croquet

parties" all the fashion; with regular clubs for playing it established in every neighborhood where there were resident gentry, and for the pleasure felt in a display of skill, combined with exercise of the intellect, this was beyond doubt, and still is, the best outdoor game ever invented. Yet County Society has quite dropped it, and taken to lawn tennis instead. No doubt their abandonment of croquet was greatly due to the implements used in playing it; these, through misconception, and the influence of the leading newspaper authority on sport, being such as to make the game about as enjoyable as that of billiards played with broomsticks for cues and cannon-shot for balls. But croquet had also got into the hands of the common people; the hoops might be seen on the grassplot of every suburban villa, and so it was no longer a pastime for the fashionables. How long lawn tennis will continue to be so it is difficult to say. Likely it will have a more extended lease of exclusiveness, from its very insipidity; the people not caring for this elaborate form of battledore and shuttlecock.

But the pastime most exclusive and recherché new in vogue with County Society is that of archery. Of late years this has been "all the rage," nearly every family of the gentry class owning bows, arrows and targets; one or more members of each belonging to an "archery club." For, although there is practice at home, the show shooting is done at club meetings, where a hundred or more of these amateur archers assemble, ladies and gentlemen in about equal numbers. Every county has its archery club—some, two or three—and the meetings are periodical, usually once a fortnight, while the fine weather lasts. A costume is worn, each club having its own, according to adoption; though the wearing it is only *de rigueur* for those who take part in the shooting; spectators being excused. The ground is sometimes in a private park belonging to one of the club's members, but as often in a large pasture field chartered for the purpose and situated centrally, so as to be most convenient for all. On the day of contest the targets are set up, and a large marquee erected to eat luncheon in, or retreat to in case of rain. Sometimes the members bring their own materials of lunch with them; and sometimes a caterer provides the spread for all, charging so much a head, as previously arranged. A band of music is also engaged, which gives additional zest to the day's enjoyment. The targets are placed in two rows, at about 100 yards apart, facing one another. Each row will have five or six of them, so that several archers may be shooting together, thus saving time. Time is also economized by having the two sets of targets, which are shot at alternately, the shooters after spending the allotted number of arrows passing from one to the other, while the scattered shafts are being collected. I need not enter into the details of this pastimes, which in itself is one of the poorest, and, except for the accompaniments and surroundings, would be dull indeed. In these, however, there is a certain presumable relief, especially if the archery ground be in some picturesque spot, as that of the club to which I myself belong—the "Royal Forest of Dean Archers." Its place of meeting is in the heart of the forest, where there is an open glade of green pasture large enough for the practice; and with the costumed archers of both sexes, each armed with a long, slender bow and quiver of arrows, the white tent, with its ornamental flags, a circle of well-dressed spectators, and the band discoursing sweet music—all form an imposing sylvan scene; its grandeur further heightened by an array of carriages in the background, with servants in gay and varied liveries loitering beside them. If the day be fine, the luncheon is set out on a long table *al fresco*, and the archers, with their friends, seated around it, their liveried servants in waiting behind, offer another tableau of an original kind. And there is yet another to succeed, when the shooting has recommenced. Then the said servants take the chairs lately occupied by their masters, to make finish of the debris of cold ham, fowl and pigeon pie, with such heel-taps as may be found in wine bottles.

It might be supposed that an archery meeting, with such displays, would attract many spectators of the common people.

But, however attractive to them, they will not be there, save some half-dozen or so of the daring, unabashed kind. For although the place be unenclosed, and free to the public, there is a tacit understanding that the assemblage is a private one, confined to the archers and their friends, and all uninvited people would be looked upon as intruders. Indeed, the invitations, given by members of the club themselves, are limited to a very few—the number fixed, and in some cases extended only to guests staying at their houses. Nearly all of County Society belongs to archery clubs; some ambitious Apollos and Dianas holding membership in two or more of them. The attendant expenses are not great; usually an admittance fee of a guinea, with the annual subscription of half a guinea. The fund thus raised goes to providing the tent, targets and music; the luncheon, of course, being a separate affair, as the costume dress, which last, as already said, is optional, save to those who shoot. But slight as the expenditure, archery clubs are not easy of entrance, the black ball jealously excluding everybody who has not also the entrée of society's charmed circle.

Another and the more ordinary of summer recreations, in which County Society indulges is the "garden-party," or, as it is sometimes termed, "at home." This is altogether a private affair, and calls not for a particular description, only to say that the giver of it invites a larger number of guests than he or she would were it a dinner. Of more miscellaneous character, too, since the garden-party may include poor relations of a distant kinship, with acquaintances not deemed eligible to the intimacy of the dinner-table. For all such it is a convenient way of giving satisfaction and clearing off old scores of indebted hospitality. An inexpensive one, too, since the fare set forth is of the "light refreshment" kind, costing little—cakes and confectionary of various sorts, with blanc-mange, jellies and ice-cream. For drink, the abominations of claret and champagne cups, if not their more abominable counterfeits in *vin ordinaire* and cider.

At most or all of these garden parties there are archery, lawn tennis and croquet; this last still retaining its corner, though despised and neglected. But the chief occupation of the garden-party is to spend an hour or two in conversation, idle or otherwise. In a sense they have their uses; bringing people together who live many miles apart, and may not have other opportunity of meeting. Sometimes this convention is of the closest kind; the treacherous climate of England making it so. A garden-party not unfrequently gets under a deluge of rain, when all have to retreat inside, filling up drawing and dining-rooms, hall, corridors, with every sheltered space available. And often the guest have to stay there till the orthodox hour of breaking up, between 6 p.m. and 7; the time of commencement being 3 p.m. on the invitation card, but nearer 4 for arrival.

It is well on in the summer, nearing autumn, when garden-parties are most given; fruit being then ripe and figuring largely in the *meau* set before the guests; another inexpensive convenience, too, the host or hostess having grown it in their own orchard, or under glass. Grander and more potential the display when it consists of pineapples, peaches, melons and products of a tropical kind. But in the gardens of the English aristocracy all these are grown, some of them even superior to what nature produces in her unaided efforts.

In the flush season of garden-party giving there will be several of them within the week; more or less according to the number of gentry resident in the neighborhood. Other people, the *hoi polloi*, know little about these goings on, only being made aware of them by seeing an unusual number of carriages whirled along the roads toward a common centre, each with a contingent of ladies and gentlemen, the former in full finery of dress, whatever the wear of the latter. And oh! the envy which boils up in the heart of many such spectators, believing as they do that the actors in the scene are on their way to an earthly paradise! Could they enter it, and become acquainted with its realities—all its hollowness and insipid assumptions—they would be better contented with their lot, humble as it is.

XIII.
County Society in Winter.

Original publication date: June 25, 1882.

In late summer and autumn county society sojourns for a while by the seaside, at the fashionable watering-places. There are also inland towns with mineral springs, frequented by a portion of it at this time of year, while another section seeks recreation abroad in a short tour, or stays at one of the noted Continental resorts; yachting trips, too, are indulged in by those of its members owning yachts, or having friends who own them. With the 12th of August there is another exodus from county houses, chiefly of gentlemen; that being the day on which grouse-shooting legally begins. To kill a grouse before would not only be unsportsmanlike, but might get the slaughterer fined, whether he held a game license or not. For all, at the earliest hour on the morning of the 12th large numbers of these birds appear on the stalls of the London game-dealers, and considering the distance they must have come to get them, infringement of the statute is an obvious inference. In England, grouse abounds only in a few of the northern shires, while also inhabiting the mountains of Wales and Ireland. Scotland, however, is the chief source of supply; and for several days preceding the 12th the platforms of railway stations, on lines leading to the north, exhibit all the paraphernalia of sport; guns in cases; dogs of the spaniel and pointer breed being thrust into the railway boxes prepared for them; gamekeepers garbed in the orthodox velveteen coat, breeches and garters, with the sportsmen themselves moving about in every variety of shooting costume.

As it is something of a boast to go grouse-shooting, it need hardly be said that the sport is an expensive one; large sums of money being paid as rental for grouse-preserves, or "grouse-moors," as they are commonly called. I may also mention there deer-stalking, the two sports often being conjoined in the Highlands and islands of Scotland, where extensive tracts of woodland are kept stocked with deer for this especial purpose. And so fashionably popular has it been of late years, that many a Scotch "laird," formerly the penniless proprietor of only worthless wastes, or unprofitable sheep-runs, is now enjoying a handsome income from these, maintained as "grouse-moors" and "deer-forests." Such are rented, or purchased outright; in either case fabulous prices are asked and freely given for them; some renting as high as from £5,000 to £10,000 a year, with the selling price in proportion. Rumor has it that there is frequent trickery in their letting; the preserves being found not half so well stocked as represented in the newspaper advertisement which has drawn attention to them. I can myself speak of a transaction of purchase which certainly bears this color; one of my acquaintances, a wealthy young baronet, being the victim. He bought a Scotch island, well wooded and abundantly supplied with deer, roebuck, grouse and other game. So far the representation was correct; but when the purchase was completed and the money paid—£70,000—he found a hole in the bottom of his bargain not set forth on the bill of sale, namely, the ugly fact that landing could only be made on the island when the wind blew from a certain quarter, which it often did not for weeks! And once upon it, there was an equal difficulty getting off again; the goings to and comings from this happy (?) hunting ground being alike dependent on the caprice of weather. My friend is still "lord of the isle," finding it a white elephant on his hands, more costly than Jumbo has been to Mr. Barnum; and for the sake of your enterprising showman, let me hope also less profitable.

On each of these grouse-shooting and deer-stalking estates there is a habitable residence; sometimes only a "box" or lodge, but often a goodly mansion, with stabling, coach-house, servants' quarters and such like accommodation. In the latter case the sportsman will have a number of friends staying with him as guests, ladies as well as gentlemen, the gentlemen taking part in the sport, the ladies being occasional spectators of it, while the evening hours, devoted to festivity, are enlivened by their presence. Many a matrimonial affair, with some flirting not meant for matrimony, has had commencement, or made progress, upon the moors and mountains of Scotland. Hilarity there rules the hours all round, and the life while it lasts is cheerful, even delectable. But its delights are not exclusive to county society, nor gentry of any kind. Indeed it is doubtful whether half of those who go grouse-shooting and deer-stalking are of the aristocracy class. Plutus, from London, Liverpool, Manchester and other prosperous centres of trade, enjoys these fashionable sports too; and can as well pay for them; while to the canny Scotch laird, his money is just as good as that of peer or prince. So the laird pockets it, and after paying gamekeepers, watchers, "gillies" and the like, finds a surplus to the good, enabling him to maintain state such as his ancestors never had nor dreamt of.

Perhaps the most noteworthy annual event in the life of county society occurs on the 1st of September, facetiously termed St. Partridge's Day. However occupied elsewhere, or wherever scattered about, at this time there is a general gathering home to enjoy the sport of partridge shooting, not legally allowable before the first day of September. The reason of its commencing later than grouse-shooting is partly from the mountain bird having its brood earlier ready for the gun than that of the plain, and partly because partridges cannot be followed into the standing corn without damage to the crop. So they get grace until this is cut down, leaving them only the stubble and turnip fields for sheltering cover—no protection at all against the keen scent of the pointer; indeed worse than none, because of its betraying them into a false security. During September, one passing along the roads of rural England will see every her and there in the adjacent fields a party engaged in partridge-shooting; or as it is more commonly called by themselves, bird-shooting, the partridge, in sportsman's phraseology, bearing the distinctive title, "bird." There will be two or three gentlemen, usually attired in shooting jackets of Tweed cloth, armed with double-barrelled breech-loaders, and attended by a gamekeeper, with one or more assistants for retrieving and carrying the killed game. When gentlemen of the *haut ton*, or county society, their attire is of the simplest kind, the elaborate showy get-up of the French and other Continental sportsmen being affected in England only by those *not* to the manner born. These partridge-shooters go tramping through the "stubs" and "Swedes," their well-trained dogs quartering the ground in front, till one or other makes a "point." Then there is a drawing up to where the covey is squatted; not in any excited haste, for that would be unsportsman like; then a signal word is given to "flush" the birds, after which the guns go banging, barrel after barrel, a partridge falling to almost every shot, for the men who have fired them are well practised in this sort of gunning, none knowing or doing it better.

Partridge-shooting lasts throughout all the winter, but by the end of September the birds are pretty well thinned off, and have become wild, so that shooting them is no longer a thing of *battue* and slaughter. Just then, however, comes in another specialty of sport, still more deserving to be thus characterized—pheasant-shooting. Its legalized day of commencement is the 1st of October, the later date partly due to a similar cause as that which affects the comparative periods when grouse and partridges may be slain. With this sport there is also some change of scene, from open fields to woodlands; the pheasant being a bird of the covert. And there are fewer sportsmen who have the chance of indulging in it; any farm-land producing coveys of partridges, while the pheasant is only found in the copses and covers chiefly grown to give it habitat, and only maintained on the estates of the wealthy. For this reason pheasant-shooting is esteemed among the most aristocratic of home sports; but neither is it exclusive to the aristocracy. Plutus can play at it too, and does; all over the country both pheasant and partridge shootings being, as nearly everything else, obtainable for money. They are constantly advertised "To Let," the price varying according to the shire or district; ruled also by the probable quantity of game existent on any particular estate. In the home counties," as those immediately around London are called, the exclusive right of shooting over ordinary farm-land costs about a shilling an acre; though the farmer is never or rarely the beneficiary granter of it, but his landlord. The right extends only to a single year, and as upon the sportsman himself devolves the additional expense of looking after the game, in the way of preserving it, the shooting costs him much more. Nor does the shilling an acre apply to regularly preserved estates, with coppice-woods for pheasant covers; these are rentable too, but of course at a higher figure. Remote from the metropolis and the large provincial towns, shooting may be had at more moderate prices; still, not without payment of something. For there is no spot, not a foot of territory in all England, but has its owner jealous of every right appertaining to it, and zealous in guarding them to the ultimate end. Disputes about the ownership of game, furred, feathered or finned, are of almost daily occurrence, the cause often trifling and ludicrous, but leading to serious results—lawsuits in which the expenses and costs far exceed the value of the commodity in litigation. As an example, I may quote a case, that for some years past has been making much stir in my own county, and several others adjacent. I reside in Herefordshire, on the banks of the river Wye, a "salmon stream," from which the fish usually taken are only a few hundred, and worth less than the same number of pounds sterling. Yet, from disputes between the upper and lower proprietors of the fishing rights—for these are property belonging to the owners of the land through which the river runs—there has been more ink spilled and paper wasted, in the pamphlet and newspaper line, than would buy up all the salmon likely to be caught out of the Wye for years to come. And this without including the cost of several expensive Government commissions sent down to adjudicate on the case, still not satisfactorily settled! Part of this cost, too, comes out of the pockets of a taxpaying people, who have no more interest in the Wye salmon than if they were so many sprats! But such is the nature of game and fish rights, with their protection and preservation all over England.

While pheasant-shooting is in progress the houses of the country gentry, especially the grander ones, are filled with guests; gentlemen invited to take part in the sport, and ladies who at midday meet them at some appointed place by the cover's side, there to eat luncheon *al fresco*, drink champagne and enjoy themselves generally. Under these circumstances, pheasant-shooting is certainly a pleasant pastime; yet is there something not so pleasant about it, indeed almost repulsive—the butchery of the birds. For it is often neither more nor less than this, the pheasants being bred and brought up nearly as tame as barn-door fowl, to be thus ruthlessly slaughtered. During the early days of shooting them, in some preserves several hundred brace will be "bagged" daily. The reader may want to know what is done with them; perhaps supposing that the magnates to whom they belong would be above making sale of them, and likely to give all away. An erroneous supposition, however; the birds bestowed being few and far between. Underlying this English spirit, even when indulged in by the grandes of country gentry, there is a keen sense of economy, with profits when obtainable; and ruled by this, the product of each day's battue, or at least the bulk of it, is packed in hampers, and that same night dispatched by rail to the London game-dealers.

At this time of the year, the local and county races are generally held; at which the gentry show themselves, viewing the contest of equine speed from open carriages, or the tops of "drags"—those of them that have the latter. In shires where racing is still in fashion among the aristocracy, there will be a grand array of such vehicles, extending along the edge of the course, each provided with the materials for a luxurious luncheon. This sport—if sport it can be called—is mostly promoted by the men who hunt;

and having a fastish flavor about it, with the taint of the betting ring, is not so much patronized by county society as might be supposed, at least not by the more respectable section of it. Once universally popular, of late years it seems to be dwindling away. And well if it do, since it is nothing but a source of corruption and ruin—a pastime for gambler and blacklegs.

It is in the winter season that county society gives its grandest dinners, with now and then a ball at the bigger houses. Sometimes it is a fancy ball, and there are also private theatricals and charade-acting. But the great dancing event of the year is the "County Ball," which is only annual and comes off when the Christmas festivities are well over. It is usually given in the "Shire-hall" of the county town, and is the exclusive of exclusives, no one being admitted who is not of the "blue blood." Stay! I have made an erroneous assertion, I had forgotten Plutus!

The county hall is under the control and management of gentlemen stewards, a dozen or more of them, all of first position in society. They canvass the credentials of those to be admitted, and a stranger who may have late settled in the county becomes aware of his eligibility by receiving a printed circular, announcing the time and place of holding the ball, the price of admission tickets and from whom they are to be had. This holds good for an invitation, which the receiver may accept at his pleasure with all the members of his family. Of course the circulars are only sent to those whom the stewards have decided to be of the elite.

There is also the "Hunt Ball," given annually in every shire; a select affair, too, but not quite so exclusive as the County one. It is got up by the members of the fox-hunting clubs, and, as many individuals patronize the sport who are not in the English sense gentlemen, there needs more latitude in the admission. Where these excluded from the balls their support given to the hunt would be lost. Hunting itself is of course one of the winter amusements of England, in which county society bears a principal part. Conducted as it is, it almost forms a specialty of English rural life; and for this reason needs greater space given it than the present article allows.

XIV.
Hunting and Hounds.

Original publication date: July 2, 1882.

Hunting is, par excellence, the sport of England, and for systemized hunting with hounds England is par excellence the country of the sport. In no other is it carried on with such zeal, and at so great cost; and none is there where so many people approved of or take part in it. Proof of this will be found in the fact that throughout the kingdom there are no less than 350 packs of hounds, averaging between thirty and forty couples each, to wit: 15 of staghounds, 171 of foxhounds, 136 of harriers, 19 of beagles, with a few packs of other hounds. Greyhounds are also kept in large numbers all over the country; while certain breeds of terriers are trained as aids and adjuncts of the sport. Of the packs England of course possesses the majority, though Ireland, up to the Land League agitation, had its full quota proportioned to population. Scotland and Wales, from their mountainous nature, are in a manner precluded from this specialty of sport, the former having in all only eight packs of foxhounds, with one of harriers and one of beagles.

Some packs are the property of and maintained by private individuals; rich magnates to whom money is of slight consequence when weighed against the grandeur of owning and keeping up a pack of hounds. These are few, however, most being "subscription packs," supported by regular subscribers who are members of the Hunt, with occasional voluntary contributions from outsiders. But there is often a deficiency of cash, with much strain in meeting the expenses of the year; so much, that now and then a pack falls to pieces, the hunt is given up, and the hounds, with horses and other belongings, are sold off under the hammer.

After a time a fresh spirit of hunting zeal may spring up in the abandoned district, from new men of wealth coming to reside in it, when an effort will be made to resuscitate the hunt, which is generally successful. Every year some parks are broken up, and others either reestablished or for the first time got together.

The cost of keeping a pack of hounds varies much, and is dependent on several circumstances, as the number and character of the official staff of management, the frequency with which the pack is hunted, and, to some extent, its size. Each pack has a Master, presumptively a gentleman in the social sense of the word; and the office is supposed to be honorary—at least there is no fixed salary attached to it. But as the Masters have sole control and expenditure of the fund, it is pretty well understood that they recoup themselves not only for outlays of money, but for time and trouble too. Most of them certainly do so, though not all; some being losers by it, for glory's sake. In all cases, however, there is an understanding that the Master shall not be at any expense for his mount; this being provided for him, and of the best. But the usual method is: Before undertaking to hunt a pack of hounds, the Master that is to be demands a certain fixed sum subscribed and put into his hands, sufficient to cover all expenses, which he also binds himself to meet. With this money he can deal as it seems best to him; expend it all and hunt the pack well; or be stingy and save some of it for himself, turning out the hounds in a un-handsome manner. There are ever Masters of this kind, though not many.

After a pack has been established, kennels built, hounds and horse of the hunt purchased, the chief outlay is in the pay of the subordinate officials and the keep of the horses, as also that of the hounds themselves. In addition to the Master, ever pack has a Huntsman and Whip; in the majority of cases tow of the latter, and in noted hunts, as the Pytchley, Berkley, Quorn and Belvoir, there or ever more. Attached to such packs there is also a "Kennel Huntsman," whose duty consists in looking after the hounds at home; and if foxhounds there will be a numerous tribe of "earthstoppers," needing to be remunerated for the quaintly curious part they are called upon to play. All these men receive a handsome wage, the huntsman and whips well earning it. For not only is their work heard, but they must be the best of riders, able to keep well up to the hounds, and so risking their necks every day they are out. As most packs hunt from three to five days a week, some even six, it will be seen that the calling of either huntsman or whip is no sinecure. The amount required for the maintenance of an ordinary pack may be roughly estimated at £1,500 a year' but there are large establishments where this is far exceeded, and many small ones conducted economically at much less expense—say one-half for the average. Of course these figures have nothing to do with the cost of establishing the pack which calls for a considerable outlay on the items above adduced. When the hunting days are frequent, Master, Huntsman and Whips require several horses each; so making the expense all the greater.

In the order of English *venerie*, stag-hunting might be supposed to have first place, and do it has theoretically. Practically, however, it is rather looked down upon as a sport chiefly indulged in by the denizens of London. Of the fifteen packs of staghounds, more than half belong to the home counties; that is, are kennelled and hunted within a radius of twenty or thirty miles around the metropolis. And the hunted animal is a half-domesticated deer, caught up out of some park, taken in a covered cart to the place of "meet," and there let off, with a few seconds grace given it for start, when the hounds are laid on after. As a rule the creature will run wildly and distractedly across country, affording a chase of ten or fifteen miles; at length to bring up in some lake, or it may be a duck-pond, there standing at bay, and perhaps killing two or three of the hounds. But sometimes it obstinately refuses to leave the spot where uncarted, or will lope off in a sulky, lazy way; to come to again in the nearest ditch, so disappointing the expectations of the "field." No without reason, therefore, is this sport sneeringly called "calf-hunting."

The most noted of these deer-hunting packs is that known as Her Majesty's staghounds, generally supposed to be the private property of the Queen, and kept up at her expense; an erroneous supposition, as they are maintained at the cost of the Nation. And no slight cost either—their Master, styled "Master of the Buckhounds," being a high-salaried official and big figure of court retinue; while a numerous array of understrappers is paid out of the same pocket. There is no grumbling, however, as these hounds are admittedly hunted *pro bono publico*. They are kennelled at Ascot Heath, near Windsor, and hunt twice a week during the hunting season; their places of meet being chiefly in the shires of Berks and Bucks, west of London, and at convenient distance from it to accommodate the cockney Nimrods. A favorable day with "Her Majesty's:" will show a field of perhaps 200 horsemen; more if a Prince or other grand dignity is expected to be present, with a sprinkling of the female element also on horseback. Three-fourths will be in orthodox hunting costume; scarlet swallow-tailed cost, helmet-shaped, hat or cap, white breeches and top boots; the officials of the hunt wearing tunics thickly garnished with gold lace, and looking like so many band-masters. The other fourth of the assembled riders will be dress in a variety of styles, but all breeched, booted and spurred, and all, or nearly all, well mounted, some of them splendidly, while an array of open carriages is drawn up on the ground, with other gentlemen and ladies who have come to witness the "uncarting." The spectacle is certainly imposing; and, to judge by the get-up of the scarlet-coated hunters, one might imagine them the very "nobs" of English aristocracy. Not a bit of it; five out of six of them are London tradesmen, stockbrokers or merchants; while most of the uncostumed, and some of the costumed too, are butchers, tavern and livery-stable keepers, horse dealers, with not a few of them arrant "copers." The greater number of these gentry are there with no thought of the chase or its enjoyment, but to show off their nags, and so to get sale for them. Many a horse changes hands in the hunting field. The other staghound packs that hunt in the home counties, are attended by a very similar following; though it is somewhat different with those in the distant shires, where the cockney element does not visibly predominate.

Fox-hunting, however, is the specialty of chase most in vogue and general practice; as may be inferred from the number of packs devoted to it. They are distributed all over the country, every shire having one or more of them; the number dependent on circumstances, such as the adaptability of the ground for hunting, and also for harboring foxes, with the inclination of the resident gentry and that of the people—more especially farmers—for the sport. Each pack has its own hunting district, with limits well defined and tacitly understood as taboo to any other. And in all these are woods and coverts where Reynard is not only allowed to live a short life, but zealously propagated and tenderly nursed, to be afterward torn to pieces. The number of foxes annually killed in England by hounds is something almost incredible; some of the packs in a single season running down as many as a hundred. The sport (?) commences in the latter part of August, with what is called "cub-hunting"; and often in the first month from twenty to thirty brace of these young foxes are caught and killed by one pack; while on throughout the winter, up till spring, one or more has to die on every hunting day. But the supply is inexhaustible for when the native article fails, "pug" is imported from abroad, France furnishing large consignments.

As to the hunt itself, the mode of procedure is as follows: On the day appointed for it, or rather the day before, the "earthstoppers" of the district to be hunted receive notice to do their work; which consists of closing up the mouths of all the fox-holes in their respective neighborhoods. It is done at night, when Reynard is ranging abroad; and, returning home, he finds the door of his own house shut against him, and so is forced to seek a temporary resting-place above ground, among the bushes. Dislodged from this lair by the hounds, he has no other resource than to run for it, and no safety but in his swiftness of foot; unless, perchance, he find some "earth" negligently left unstopped, when he takes to it. But even this does not always avail him, as the burrowing terriers, with spade and pick, are brought into play, easily unearthing him, unless the place of his retreat be among rocks or the roots of a tree. If he cannot be dug out, then the hounds are taken back to cover, with the hope of finding a fresh fox and better luck in the chase of it. When the day's hunt is over the earthstoppers go their rounds again, reopen the burrows, and so leave them.

A "meet" of foxhounds, especially in one of the noted hunting shires, is a picturesque affair, and not very different from that of the staghounds already described. Often there are over an hundred horsemen in scarlet—"pink," as figuratively called—with the same motley array of butchers, tavern-keepers and horse-dealers. Hunting farmers are in greater numbers here; but these, though breeched, booted and spurred, rarely put on the "pink." One appearing in a scarlet coat is deemed something more than presumptuous. With the foxhounds too, there is usually a larger following of ladies, whose riding habits of various hues add to the picturesqueness of the assemblage. Some of them ride well up to hounds, from the "Houry! Tally-ho! Gone away!" to the "Whoo-whoop!" announcing the kill. If a lady be in at the death, it is *comme il faut* for the huntsman to present her with the fox's "brush"; the "pads" (feet) of the animal being also cut off and distributed among those who may care for them.

A much greater number of ladies follow hounds now than formerly; the Empress of Austria having made it a fashion. But however it may be with the Irish, the farmers of Cheshire have no desire ever to see this Imperial Diana again; as her presence in their county brought upon them an invasion of rough riders from Manchester, Liverpool and other large Lancashire towns, often to the number of 300, breaking down their fences and trampling their pasture fields into beaten paths. They in fact dread a second visit from her as a pestiferous infliction!

Time was when to be an M. F. H. (Master of Foxhounds) was esteemed the *ne plus ultra* of honors; an office for which only men of patrician birth were eligible. It is not so now, at least in many of the shires. In some of them masterships even go begging; to be taken up by anyone having the inclination with the money—this last, or rather the want of it, being the key to their present disfavor. And they are so taken up, all over the country; these modern M. F. H.'s affecting the ancient fox-hunting squire and playing the part in grander style than ever did he. For they not only contribute largely to the support of the pack, but give sumptuous hunting breakfasts at their houses; the *elite* inside quaffing claret and champagne, while outside on the lawn the *hoi polloi* are regaled with bread, beef and beer.

But though fox-hunting, as regards its master ship, may not be what it was, it is still a highly aristocratic sport; and the repute of having taken part in it a thing of pride and boast even greater than grouse-shooting or deer stalking. As proof of and illustrating this there is a phase of life supremely ridiculous—that of pretended fox-hunting. In London it exists where there are houses known as "splashing houses," their métier being to bespatter gentlemen dressed in hunting costume with mud, so that they may present themselves at their clubs or elsewhere as if just returned from the hunting field! Nay, more, these splashers even deal with distinct kinds of mud, as that of Northampton, should the gentleman wish to have it thought he has been hunting with the famed Pytchley pack, or the mud of Leicestershire if he prefer to have been out with the not less famous Quorn! I am positively assured that such establishments exist; nor have I any reason to doubt it. Instead, the reverse; having myself known men in London to put on shooting costume, and make public appearance in it, who never took out a game license or carried a gun! Others too, who were accustomed to show themselves last at night in fall dinner dress, as though they had been "dining out," when they had only made a frugal and solitary repast at some obscure chop-house.

XV.
Hunting, with Harriers, Beagles, Otterhounds and Greyhounds

Original publication date: July 9, 1882.

Though among English field sports hare hunting holds inferior rank to either stag or fox hunting, still it is in large practice; as may be inferred from the number of packs devoted to this specialty of chase. There are 136 of regular harriers, with 19 of beagles and beagle-harriers; in all 155, or nearly as many as the packs of foxhounds. To such of THE TRIBUNE's readers are unlearned in canine lore, I may observe that these different sorts of hounds are only varieties of the same animal, produced by time, breeding and training; their points of distinction being size and strength, combined with powers of endurance, as also keenness of scent and swiftness of foot. Size, however, is their chief distinctive characteristic; and in this they are almost regularly graduated, from the stalwart staghound down to the diminutive beagle of ten inches in height; some even less, as the "lapdog beagles" of Queen Elizabeth, that could find sleeping room inside a man's glove! Of course, none such are now employed in the hunting field; though there are several packs in which the standard of height are only ten inches, with others—pure, beagles, too—where it is nearer twenty. Nor is the staghound of the pack, that properly so called, and now nearly extinct. Instead, the animal used in the chase of the semi-domesticated deer may be regarded as only a larger variety of foxhound; the harrier a smaller one; and the beagle smallest of all. The packs of harriers, however, are frequently composed in part of foxhounds, just as in many beagle packs, there is an admixture of harriers.

For a time confining my remarks to these last, it is to be said that a pack of harriers is also less in individual numbers than one of foxhounds; twenty couples being rather above the average of the former, and not half as many as in the latter. The cost of their establishment and maintenance is therefore correspondingly less; and as harriers are rarely hunted more than two days in the week, this further reduces the expense, by the fewer horses required to mount Master, Huntsman and Whip. Only in a few packs is there a "Second Whip"; while in nearly half of them the Master is himself Huntsman, by this doubling or role saving an outlay on the paid professional. Three hundred pounds per annum will maintain a respectable hunt of harriers, thus economically managed; though there are some conducted on a more expensive scale. As in the case of foxhounds, nearly all are "subscription packs," the Masters undertaking to hunt them for a fixed sum, guaranteed and made up by the members of each particular hunt, with the aid of voluntary contributors. But, as with foxhounds also, some packs are private property, their owners keeping them up partly for the pleasure of the sport, but also with an idea of grandeur and popularity.

The less expense attending a pack of harriers is one reason why there are so many of them; for hare-hunting is not thought nearly so much of as fox hunting. But there are districts without the money strength to support a hunt of the latter, though able to afford enough for one of the former. Besides, foxes may be few and far between, while hares are abundant everywhere, so that n harrier hunting a "blank" day would be the rarest of exceptions.

The following of a harrier pack is very different from that seen after foxhounds, there being fewer men on horseback, and these less showily attired. Some may be in hunt costume, too, but the "pink," as the orthodox color for harriers is green. This in silk velvet or fine melton cloth, with gold buttons, is becoming enough, though of less brilliant display than the scarlet of the foxhunter. Moreover, of late years a uniform in harrier-hunting is affected only by the few; a "field" often showing only the Master and Huntsman in uniform, all the other wearing coats of the ordinary cut and color. Breeches, however, are indispensable, either buckskin or cord, with top boots, or what answers equally as well, though not so stylish, short leather leggings, close-fitting around ankle and calf. Many who ride with harriers wear these last; economy compelling; for even in England—country of low-priced apparel—a pair of top boots is a somewhat costly equipment. A paucity of long-skirted riding habits is also observable in a "field" of harriers; for although ladies hunt with these hounds too, they are never in such numbers as with foxhounds. Indeed, neither are gentlemen, in the "society" sense; the greater number of those who practise harrier hunting being men of the middle class, with some belonging to a still lower one.

In most parts of the country farmers make up the chief following of harriers, especially the younger ones of sporting proclivity. Though hares are under the protection of the Game statutes, no game license is required for hunting them with hounds, and therefore no expense attends it save subscription to the hunt fund; and even this is more voluntary that compulsory. Besides, farmers are let off easily in consideration of their favoring the sport; which without their countenance would not prosper, if possible to carry it on. For the wear and tear of their horses, as already hinted, they generally look for recoupment by their sale to such young "swells" of the gentry class as may be met in the field, wanting a mount better than that they are on. So to the farmers hunting is often a profit as well as sport. Despite these temptations, however, the majority take no part in it, while many go dead against it. They have its *per contras* to consider, in broken-down fences and trampled fields, the latter often under crop. True, they can recover for the actual damage done, though not for trespass; the unwritten law of long custom debarring them from that. And public opinion almost equally hinders their having recourse to the former, hunting is so popular with the masses. Some farmers, however, brave all this and stand up for their rights, at the risk, indeed the certainty, of being called churlish. Hence collisions now and then occur between them and the hunters, resulting in lawsuits with claims for damages. Sometimes it is a case of assault, when a hot-blooded Nimrod has his horse seized by the bridle, and lays the lash or stock of his hunting-crop over the shoulders of Hodge trying to detain him.

From all this it may be inferred that great efforts are made to conciliate the farmer, and get him to go in for hunting, if not already addicted to it. Whatever damage he may have sustained in spoiled fences or the like is made good to him out of the hunt fund. And should he have a claim for poultry carried off by the prowling fox, it will be readily conceded and liberally adjusted in the same way. Anything to keep him from complaining. Were it not so, Reynard would be often found in a ditch by the woodside stark and stiff, as he sometimes is found, victim to a bit or beef or mutton saturated with strychnine.

As further propitiation of the farmer, and winning him over to favor the chase, at all hunt-dinners he is the subject of much flattery, combined with cajolery. In the speeches there made he is told what an advantage hunting is to the country, more especially to himself; how it promotes his interest in the sale of horses, hay and oats; as also encourages gentry to reside in his neighborhood, from whom other benefits may accrue to him. All this is said in serious sober earnest, as though it were not the funniest of farces! And the game is repeated over and over again, year after year, ultimately *ad nauseum*; a pitiful commentary on a country dependent on such aids to prosperity. In point of fact they are more drawback than advantage to it; as hunting encourages idleness among the working classes, if not something worse.

In its mode of procedure, hunting with harriers presents some points of difference from that with foxhounds. The "meet" is much the same, the day and hour being advertised beforehand in the local papers, with the place; this is usually some crossroads or country tavern. Between 10 and 11 a.m. the hounds are brought upon the ground by the huntsman and whip, generally accompanied by the master. There they are kept for some fifteen or twenty minutes, awaiting the arrival of the other horsemen and lady riders who are to compose the mounted field. Sometimes a carriage or two will show upon the ground, with lady friends of the master, or other gentlemen of the hunt. Harrier meets, however, are rarely thus graced and honored; the spectacle being less attractive than when they are stag or foxhounds. But there will be a large muster of men on foot, with boys, even women and girls, all looking forward to great enjoyment when the hounds are cast off. After due grace has been given for the laggards to get up, the casting off is done in some near field, where there may be hope of finding a hare. With foxhounds it would be in a wood or cover; so those who hunt with harriers have a better opportunity of witnessing them at their work; not only the search and quarterings, but the chase itself. For at the "Tally-ho!" Reynard is off, and soon out of sight, with little hope of being seen again, at least by the foot following; while the "View-halloo!" which signals the start of the hare, imparts no such cheerless prospect. Instead, from a convenient hilltop a view of the whole chase can often be commanded from beginning to end, whether it terminate in a kill or in Puss outwitting the hounds by a double, or temporary retreat into some thick covert of bushes. For this reason, though hunting with harriers may be an inferior sport to fox-hunting as regards those on horseback, it is certainly not so for the foot-following, but rather the reverse. More especially is this the case in districts of coverless open country, where the hare will often lead the hounds a long continuous chase; as, for instance, in treeless Ireland. There I remember having ridden after harriers in pursuit of the same hare from 11 a.m. till 2 in the afternoon; not in a straight run, but around hills, with many turnings and doublings, as also intervals of lost scent, in all of which an Irish hare will display quite as much cunning as a fox, and as frequently throw hounds outs. I may observed that the Irish hare is of a different species from that of England, and although not so long in the legs, is, I believe, swifter of foot. If so, it would be in consonance with the Darwinian theory of adaptation to circumstances; since in a country where there is little or no cover to conceal the chased animal, only by swiftness can it escape.

Hunting with beagles is regarded as a specialty of the chase even lower in degree than hunting with harriers. Some, however, follow it with zest, and there are certain circumstances in its favor. A pack of these Lilliputian hounds costs little in the keeping; and from their slow pace they can be followed on foot, as they often are; thus saving horse expenses. They are also employed in hunting rabbits, that is, running them out of cover into the open, so that sight might be got of them for the gun. Many of the so-called beagle packs, however, as already said, are more than half harriers, some indeed altogether so, and usually distinguished as beagle-harriers.

Otter-hunting is another English sport in which hounds are employed, these being of a small breed, and rough-coated, the long hair making them better fitted for enduring cold while in the water. But indeed most hounds can be trained to otter hunting; and in the packs—of which there are several throughout the country—many are only harriers, or foxhounds, that have not proved up to much in the nobler chase, and so got disbanded from it. The otter still exists in many English streams; though it is more abundant in those of Wales and Scotland, where most of the packs are kept up. As its hunt is necessarily along a river's bank, and generally over a rough ground, horses are not available for it; the following being all afoot. Sometimes the otter-hunters appear in costume, though there is not regulation dress either in cut or color as with harriers and fox-hounds. Each hunt has its own, adopted according to fancy, just as with archery clubs. Pictures of otter-hunting show men armed with spears, and usually the otter hoisted upon one. This is a thing of the past; or, when designed to represent a scene of present time, it is only an artist's fancy. The modern otter-hunter of England carries no spear, not anything of the sort.

Last in the list of English venerie is hunting with greyhounds, which is technically termed "coursing," the greyhounds themselves being in like manner called dogs, not hounds, by those who follow the sport. Of this no description need here be given, as doubtless most Americans are familiar with it. They may not know, however, to what extent it is practised in England; nor were it easy to say how many greyhounds are kept for it, since they are not in packs, but of private ownership, and distributed everywhere. But the number must be enormous, as in every parish there are several, and in every shire hundreds, while the towns and villages have their quota as well. Tradesmen given to sporting much affect them, and farmers still more. The expense is trifling, only the cost of the "dog's" keep, or a couple of them, with the dog-tax of seven shillings and sixpence, which has to be paid for any other kind of canine. Thus the sport is within reach of anyone having leave to "course" over land, a privilege not very difficult to obtain. But there is a factor at the bottom or coursing very different from any ideas of sport; the same which underlies nearly every pastime in England—that is, gambling. Writers moralize over the hells of Homburg and Monaco, turning up Pecksniffian noses, as though shocked at the infamy of such institutions in other lands; while in England itself gaming is a passion universal as anywhere, and as universally indulged in, with all its cheating and trickery. In a respectable way, though—the word respectable is a favorite—and not by card-playing and dice-throwing; instead, Englishmen make the swift foot of the greyhound, as the hoof of the race-horse, subservient to it. So there are "coursing matches," day and daily all over the land, with large sums of money laid upon them; a couple of greyhounds unleashed after a poor hare to run the creature to death—spectacle affecting as cruel. All this is recorded in due form and solemnity, not only in newspapers specially devoted to sport, but those highest in the ranks of journalistic literature—aye, in all of them. It seems a mental pabulum as necessary to the people of England as the daily column of Court news with the doings of Royalty and Nobility.

Houses of Parliament, circa 1890; courtesy Library of Congress, Washington, D.C.

XVI.
The Representation in Parliament

Original publication date: July 16, 1882.

In previous articles I have treated of English rural life only its social aspects; let me now speak of it politically, beginning with the highest of its *haute politique*—representation in Parliament.

The members who more especially represent it are termed "country members," to distinguish them from those who site for the corporate towns or boroughs, called "borough members." Of the former there are 283, and the latter 360, which with nine representing universities make up the House of Commons—in all 652. Thus, in point of numbers, the English people are better represented in their National Legislature than those of the United States; but in all other respects worse—indeed, not represented at all, as I shall presently show.

Within the walls of Parliament there is no difference between a county and a borough member, either in power or privileges; the yea or nay of the one being just as good as that of the other. But whether inside or out, the county member considers himself above the borough one, and is generally regarded. Why this fancied superiority—for it is only a fancy—Americans may desire to know; all the more when told that country constituencies are not only smaller than those of many boroughs, but less intelligent and enlightened. Numbers, however, have nothing to do with it, neither has intelligence nor enlightenment; there being a factor, in the eyes of Englishmen, more powerful than all three put together—fashion. But whence and why the fashion, is the collateral question that crops up, to get answer that, from time immemorial, county constituencies have been represented in Parliament by the scions of aristocracy, while borough members may be anybody or anything, even "low-born" men, as some of them are. About the former there is a fine high-spiced flavor of patricianism, while around the latter hangs and clings the vulgar odor of democracy—as the English idea has it. Hence, to "sit for a shire," however poor or sparsely inhabited, is a prouder distinction than to be the representative of the richest and most populous borough. Under these circumstances it need hardly be said that county members are nearly all of them county magnates, and the majority of them Conservatives of the high Tory type. If professing Liberalism, it will be of the Whig specialty, which differs from Toryism in little beyond the name; neither having the slightest thought or intention of enlarging the liberties of the people, or relaxing their own grasp of sweet privileges, so long and tenaciously held. In some of the shires Toryism controls the voting strength, in others the Whig element has the upper hand; while in some it is about equally balanced between them. But whichever be in the ascendant, the Parliamentary representation of a county is practically vested in three or four of its leading families, who look upon it as a sort of heirloom and patrimonial right. When divided, the sharing is done in a friendly give-and-take way, as "you have one of the seats, I the other." For it is to be observed that most counties send two members to Parliament, some even three, while a few of the less populated ones have only a single representative.

It may be asked how the county constituencies are thus exclusively controlled by a few aristocratic families. The answer is that the bulk of country people having the franchise are tenant farmers, whose interest it is to vote as their landlords direct them. Ever hanging over their heads, as the sword of Damocles, are possibilities of increased rent, and probabilities of a back term unpaid, with visions of sales under the statute of distress, or other like disagreeables. And as their landlords are, almost to a man, territorial magnates, the central figures and strength of aristocracy itself, it will be easily understood how it is with shire representation. Just now the landed power is less than it ever has been, having received a rude shock and check from the depressed state of agriculture, which, while impoverishing the farmer, has to some extent released him from his political thralldom. A curious fact of enfranchisement and apparently a paradox this, nevertheless a substantial truth, comprehensible as the defiance born of penury and despair. With thousands of farms untenanted and begging occupation, the farmer has the whip hand of his landlord, and may vote as it pleases him. But how long will this last? Not likely for any great length of time, unless the depression itself continue. It is almost certain that a return of prosperity would reexcite land-hunger and bring things back into their old grooves and channels. So far, the political disturbance has been slight, and the change as regards Parliamentary representation scarcely appreciable.

True, not all county members are bred and born patricians; for not all of the counties are controlled by the farmers' vote. Some are in populous mining districts, while into others extend the suburbs of cities, over which tower tall smoking chimneys—the homes of manufacturers and well-to-do mechanics, also endowed with the franchise. In these the balance of voting power, wrested from patrician grasp, is in the hands of the real people. Such constituencies, however, are not numerous; and, strange to say, neither do they always favor candidates of their own social order; instead rather those of a class above them. *Ceteris paribus* the man of title—baronet, or lord—stands a better chance with them, aye, far better, than he has no handle to his name. Richard Cobden, who represented one of these piebald county constituencies—the West Riding of Yorkshire—said, and said justly, that, in this regard, society had nothing to fear from the encroachments of democracy, as "fireside jealousies"—his phrase, if I remember aright—would always restrain an undue intrusion of the proletarian element into Parliament, or other posts of honor. I had the honor of acquaintance with the great Apostle of Free Trade, and have heard this from his own lips; words made public at the time. But though that was a quarter of a century ago, they still hold good; indeed, judging by the samples of workingmen's representatives sent to Parliament, they would seem to deserve holding good. Of these there have been three or four; and one of them—Macdonald late deceased—actually counselled his constituency of coal-miners to suspend work so that coal might become scarce and dear, and as a consequence their wages get raised! The man seriously and zealously promulgated this mischievous doctrine in speeches made all over the land; in direct violation of the best known and most universally admitted principles of human economy. With such advocates the laboring-man element in Parliament is not likely to have increase; and no doubt Macdonald's example will have done something to retard it.

Just now another element is making attempt to gain a foothold within the same exalted precinct—one more special to the subject of this letter on rural life—the farmer element. The agricultural depression, giving farmers a grievance, has, as already stated, also armed them with an amount of political power; taking advantage of which four or five of them have been pitchforked into Parliament. Some of them tenant farmers too. But neither has this experiment proved a brilliant success; instead rather a dull, disappointing failure. And so will it be, until farmers learn how to select their best men to represent them. As it is, most those they have chosen are mere noisy chatterers, the product of those assemblages—possibly the most objective and useless ever known to the world—known as "Chambers of Agriculture." It need hardly be said that these farmer-members are of strong Conservative principles, indeed ultra Tory. One or two of them, supposed to be of Liberal inkling, when candidates for election, and questioned about their views, were mute as mice; knowing that to declare them were to be kept out of Parliament. And now that they are in it, there is no more heard of their Liberalism; instead their tendency to take the opposite side every day more and more shows itself. Wonderfully patriotic they are—very Chauvins—in matters of foreign policy, especially on the question of American meat. Importation of this,

THE REPRESENTATION IN PARLIAMENT

as farmers' representatives, it is their duty to opposed, whether it be alive on the hoof or dead and packed in ice. Not much concern is it to them how the poor man may need or fare without it. As M.P.'s they mix and mingle with county society, after a fashion; seeming to lose their heads at finding or fancying themselves part of it. And how county society pets and pats them on the back— these elected legislators, whom before elected it would not have deigned to notice, save by the most supercilious of nods!

It is not likely, however, things standing as they are now, that many of these representatives of agriculture and laboring interests will ever enter Parliament. For there is a bar to their admission, even more obstructive than that cited by Mr. Cobden—money. I do not mean the money qualification, of so much a year income, that being abolished, but the outlay attending an election. Whether the candidate succeed or fail, this something considerable, mounting up to many hundreds of pounds; even when the contest is conducted on the most economic principles and uncorruptedly. But it rarely is so; more generally votes having to be purchased; then it takes as many thousands to pay the bill. Few farmers' candidate can stand such expense; must less those who would represent labor; therefore the money must be mad up for them by friendly and class contribution, as in several instances it has been. But contributors to such fund are prone to become tired of it, especially with such poor returns as they have hitherto had for their outlay. So the experiment is not likely to be repeated on any large scale.

It may be wondered that such outlay is needed, and the reason asked. Will not a candidate's fame and good name, with his fitness for the office, rally around him, and bring up the polls, all who are interested in his election? They who would put this question can know little of the indifference of England's people, more especially in the rural districts, as regards their exercise of the franchise. True, it would seem otherwise, the very reverse, to one present at a contested county election. On the day of it the roads leading to the polling centres will display traffic at an unusual kind; omnibuses, flys, cabs, and ever private carriages, all plastered over with posting bills, the color of the paper blue or yellow according to the politics of the candidate they are plying for, all driven at furious speed and crammed with men in a high state of excitement. A stranger thus viewing them as they hasten toward the polling place might supposed them madly eager to exercise their right of citizenship—that little and limited one allowed them—to elect a member of Parliament. But no; they are not coaching at their own expense, not a man of them. Nor when they arrive at the polling precinct—town or village—will refreshments cost them anything. There they find tables spread and taverns running a free tap, no one exactly knowing who pays the shot. That is a secret of the electioneering agents, the lawyers engaged on each side, and the tavern-keepers; for all of whom it is a time of high jinks, a very harvest of prosperity. Nothing pleases them better than to hear of a Parliament being dissolved; for then all this nice profitable business will have to be gone over again.

Sometimes it does not end quite so agreeably; when the unsuccessful candidate thinks he can bring bribery home to the successful one. Then there is a petition to unseat the elected member, and a Commission of Inquiry appointed; when nearly always is it found that there has been something more than a free carriage ride and glass of beer at the bottom of it—in short, a money consideration given for the votes. At the last general election there was so much of this that scarce a constituency in the Kingdom escaped suspicion of having been corrupted. And a large number of them actually were corrupted; so many and so scandalous the exposures, it was found necessary to send half a dozen of the wirepullers to prison. As many hundred, equally guilty, might have been sent there; but the half-dozen wretched scapegoats were deemed valve enough to let off the steam-spurt of public indignation. Since then some legislative action has been taken to prevent such scandals in future; though it is not likely that will much avail, in a land where the voter knows his vote to be scarce worth the casting. For if ever there was a myth or misconception in the world, it is that of England having a representative form of government. That it has nothing of the kind I will give proof in another article.

Mr. Gladstone in Parliament; courtesy Library of Congress, Washington, D.C.

XVII.
The Representation in Parliament.

Original publication date: July 23, 1882.

I concluded my last letter by saying, if ever there was a myth or misconception in the world, it is that of England's having a representative form of government. The assertion may surprise the American reader, and be discredited by him, though perhaps not so much when he has heard what I have to say in support of it. I spoke of the county constituencies being almost exclusively under control a small oligarchy of aristocrats who from the time Parliaments were first instituted, ever from the *witten-gemote*, have represented them, and so come to look upon it as a sort of ancestral right. They are nearly all of the titled nobility, magnates of the first magnitude, and enter Parliament undisputedly; or if there be dispute it is among themselves, as to which of their sections—Whig or Tory—shall have the seats. But the people at large have little or no say in it, since these rural constituencies are chiefly composed of tenant-farmer who, for reasons already given, are not free in the casting of their votes.

It may be urged that they have the protection of the ballot, which should hold them scathless against landlord disfavor. It has not been found so, however; landlords having little difficulty in discovering how the cat has jumped. But even allowing these tenant-farmers full liberty of vote, with no sinister consequences to accrue, what of it? They are only a fractional part of the rural population, the bulk and body of it having no vote at all, and therefore no more to do with making the laws that govern them than the Helots of Sparta in shaping the statutes of Lacedæmon. Their only connection with law-making or law administration is the paying what it costs; and this do they, to a tune that entails on them more than half the toil and struggle of their lives. Were these non-voters less intelligent or less politically enlightened than those endowed with the franchise, there might be some excuse for its being withheld from them. But such is not the case; instead, rather the opposite, most of them being quite as capable of a rational and beneficial exercise of it as those who do exercise it, and many of them more. Among English workingmen—as mechanics and the higher grade of laborers—there are many thousands having a far clearer and wider comprehension of political truths than those who employ them. More honesty of political aim, too; being uncorrupted and untrammeled by the petty ambitions and aspirings to social rank which make many of middle class subservient to the aristocracy.

There has long been talk of admitting these non-citizens to citizenship; such bastard sort of it as English people possess in the meagre privilege of voting for a Member of Parliament. But even this is put off from day to day and year to year, while the wonder is that it could be denied them for a single hour. Possibly they may get it in time; but if they do, it will be as a bone thrown to a dog to silence his growling, and they will find it a bare, meatless one, unless there be a total rearrangement of county constituencies. As these are now, it were sheer ludicrous irony to call them a fair representation of the rural people.

Not a whit fairer or better is it with those who dwell in towns; indeed, in many cases worse. The reader will be aware that the basis of the borough franchise is different from that of the counties, and I need not enter into details. Enough to say that it also excludes the bulk of the population from this very limited exercise of civic rights. Take London itself as example, a city containing over three millions of inhabitants; not one out of every ten being entitled to vote. In like manner is it with all the large provincial towns, as Liverpool, Manchester, Birmingham, Glasgow and Edinburgh. In what sense, then, can this be regarded as a representation of the people?

THE REPRESENTATION IN PARLIAMENT

But I have not yet touched bottom. There are so many shams and deceptions in this so-called representative system, such a network of tricks and contrivances to make it utterly worthless, that time with many words is needed to reveal them. There are so many shams and deceptions in this so-called representative system, such a network of tricks and contrivances to make it utterly worthless, that time with many words is needed to reveal them. What will Americans thinks of a legislative assembly in which the vote of one man can neutralize and make nought of those of a hundred? Yet just this is done in the Parliament of England—I mean vicariously—and not exceptionally, but rather as the rule. There's many a borough whose voting constituency counts less than 300; and of course its elective majority will be a still smaller number—often not half this. Yet the member who sits for one of these has as much say in shaping the laws of England as he who represents a constituency of 15,000. It is exactly as if in the American National Legislature, the town of Newport, Rhode Island, was represented by the same number of Congressmen as the great city of New-York. Indeed the analogy does not do justice to my argument; for the people of Newport are presumably as enlightened and as capable of exercising the franchise as those of New-York, while in England it is altogether different; the voting constituencies of these miniature boroughs being often ignorant, I might almost say, in proportion to their bulk. As instance, I have a friend who sits for one of them, a very worthy gentleman, sent to Parliament over and over again by the votes of 170 men. They are all unlettered fishermen—for the privileged place is by the seaside—knowing little beyond the manipulation of their boats and nets. Yet within the walls of Parliament my friend's yea or nay—in other words the dictum of 170 ignorant fishermen—is as potential as though pronounced by the largest and most enlightened constituency in the kingdom! It is indeed a wonder how little English people are alive to the importance of an equally proportioned franchise; the great body of them being absolutely unaware of the fact that in "equal electoral districts" lie the grist and germ of all representative government. Even the Chartists, in making this one of the "six points" of their Charter, gave it a secondary place, as the despised stone of the builders, while in reality it is the true corner-stone of Liberty's fabric.

Nor have I yet shown the seamiest side of this disproportionate representation of England's people. There is another and more execrable phase of it to be exposed—the way in which these small borough constituencies are controlled. As with those of the counties, many of them are under aristocratic influence, at the beck and nod of some territorial grandee who owns them, or at least owns the houses they inhabit. It is on record that one such boasted that he could put his spaniel into Parliament; and one actually made his groom, or other underling, a member of the House of Commons, just for the joke of the thing, or the winning a wager. These are matters of past time; but the power still exist, and might be exercised to-day or to-morrow except for the fear of creating scandal. Boroughs of this kind are called "pocket boroughs," deriving their quaint appellation from the fact that the individual thus commanding their votes carries them, as it were, in his pocket. Not all the pocket boroughs, however, are under patrician control; the purse of Plutus holding influence over a goodly number of them. It is a well-known fact that there are scores of them purchasable as any other commodity of the market can be bought up, lock, stock and barrel, and are so bought. The late commission of inquiry into contested elections gave ample evidence of this, having brought to light the astounding revelation that the voters of several such boroughs—not small ones either— were bribed, almost to a man! Many of them even boasted of the large sums they had received, after stipulating for, and chaffering over them, without thought of shame or qualm of conscience.

One would naturally expect that a candidate for Parliamentary honors would be required to give some proof of his fitness for Parliamentary duties. But in boroughs like these no such qualification is needed. With, political capacity and knowledge of statesmanship—or indeed other knowledge of any useful kind—are the least and last things thought of. Money will make them take the wall; and well the man of money knows it—feels as certain of entering Parliament, if he only pay the price, as he would of an opera box by purchasing a ticket. It is simply a question of how much he is disposed to pay; and that he arranges with the electioneering agent, who in turn makes it square with the electors. There are always constituencies open to representatives of this kind, and who care for no other, and would not have any other. Nor does the candidate need to be resident among them or even have previous acquaintance with them. He may be a total stranger of unknown antecedents, brought from some distant part of the country—London or elsewhere—his first introduction to his constituency that is to be, given him by the local lawyer who acts as his electioneering agent, often only a few days before the election. But the lawyer himself has been previously made acquainted with his legislative capabilities by having heard the jingle of his gold. This communicated to the covetous constituency has a marvelous, almost magical effect, and presto! the unknown Plutus, who may be the veriest adventurer, becomes one of the Senatorial grandees of the great British Empire, on which the sun never sets!

A man without money, or of only moderate means, entering Parliament, is a thing never thought of. Such a man never thinks of it himself; whatever his self-knowledge or fitness or his ambition may be; and no more, however fit others may deem him. Even the preliminary expenses of election are sufficiently deterrent; and what must accrue after, whether elected or rejected, will further impoverish if not totally ruin him. For a poor man, there, aspiring to Parliament, the cost makes it absolutely prohibitive; and the few such sent thither are only eccentric exceptions, whose friends and admirers have stood sponsors for them, by footing the bill.

With the House of Commons composed as it is, it were the

veriest burlesque to speak of it as a representative assembly. In numbers it has enough and to spare, but in all else deficiency; and I venture the affirmation that if the names of the first thousand men met promenading the streets of London, were written upon slips of paper, thrown into a hat, and 652 of them drawn out again by blind lottery, they would be found quite as fit legislators as the elect of St. Stephen's. Perhaps better fit, for allowing them only the fair average of honesty and capacity, it is not likely there would be as many numbskulls and political empirics among them; certainly there could not be more.

In serious truth, the Parliament of England, as at present constituted, represents not the English people in any way worth their being represented. And just for this reason is it all but powerless; as the Crown and its secret advisers thoroughly well know. Indeed its action is almost as mythical as its imaginary representation. In proof of this many events of daily occurrence might be adduced; but none better demonstrating it than the vagaries of the late Lord Beaconsfield; who, as Prime Minister, for a matter of six years ruled the realm as though Parliament had been swept out of existence. With the Crown at his back and nothing else, he declared wars, and levied armies to wage them; ordered troops to be transported from India to Malta and back again; decreed an invasion of Afghanistan which, commencing with dishonor, ended in disgrace; did the same in Southern Africa, with like results—all merely to exalt himself and gratify the vainglory of the god Jingo—that malevolent divinity too oft presiding over the destinies of England. And all this murderous, wasteful work was done without the authority of Parliament, or warning given to it, even so much as saying "with your leave." When done, Parliament was merely asked to pay the bill, or rather demanded to do so, since it could not well be repudiated. The extravagant expenditure, not yet paid nor fully audited, has cost the nation some £40,000,000 sterling; a sacrifice that will bring retribution for the wrongs done, if not humiliation. And its baneful effects will hang like a millstone around England's neck for the next half century of her existence.

Speech in the House of Commons; from Robert Wilson, *The Life and Times of Queen Victoria, 1837-1897*, Vol. 4 (London: Cassell & Company, 1897).

In point of fact, the English Parliament, even allowing it to be a fair representation of the people, instead of a feeble one, is intrusted with only a portion of the national law-making; a large slice of it emanating from Privy Council; in other words, direct from the Crown. This permanent authority is endowed with all the three powers of government—judicial and executive as well as legislative—and can issue decrees or edicts, many of them relating to most important matters. They are supposed to need indorsement by the Parliament before becoming law; but there is a very loose construction put upon this leave, which is often forestalled, and usually taken for granted. The people, accustomed to be ruled by somebody above them, never call those decrees into question, but look upon them as having all the force of law. To them, the Privy Council is a mysterious but potential entity, of which they must not speak, or only with bated breath. If disposed to complain of its action, they know it to be an irresponsible power, far above and beyond the reach of their voices.

As a result of all this—its natural and logical sequence—is the indifference of the English people to exercising the franchise—a very apathy. For what interest can a man have in voting, with the conviction that his vote is not worth the casting? For it is not worth casting in England, at least as regards her Parliament; and were this dissolved to-morrow, and permanently, it would not be greatly missed.

So I once more repeat my assertion, with the hope that I have justified it, saying: If ever there was a myth or misconception in the world, it is that of England's having a representative form of government. Nor fear I to add that one nearer the opposite could not well be contrived or imagined, short of Absolutism itself.

XVIII.
School Persecution.

Original publication date: July 30, 1882.

In one of my letters giving account of the English laborer, I mentioned among his grievances the compulsory sending of his children to school. In the United States this might not be thought much of a grievance; since there the general sentiment of the people—with intelligent forecast of danger to free institutions from ignorance—favors education at all cost, even to some encroachment on individual liberty. Still, the natural rights of a man in this matter are perfectly clear, and no Government can with justice override them, by compelling him to educate either himself or his children, any more than it may force him to adopt a particular religious faith. What a Government may justly do is to exclude the uneducated from all participation in itself, even to the exercise of its first and most ordinary power—the franchise. When the great Republic enacts a law that no man in the United States be entitled to vote unless educated up to a certain standard, it will have reached the nearest to a government perfection yet known in the world. And with such bar before him, there need be no fear of the citizen declining to have his children taught; unless he be one who prefers outlawry to citizenship—a sort never likely to be so numerous as to endanger the fabric of freedom.

In England this subject has unfortunately a very different complexion, and the English laboring man regards it in a different light. He has no citizenship to aspire to, no vote, nor would any amount of education get him one. Even had he a vote, as things stand now, it would scarce be worth the casting; of which fact by a sort of intuition he is aware. This, however, is not the chief cause of his indifference to having his children go to school, a still greater one—the real grievance—being his inability to spare them for such a purpose. As I stated in the letter referred to, the English rural laborer earns barely enough to keep body and soul together, and when thrown out of work by a spell of wet weather long continued—worse still if it be one of sickness—they often come nigh falling apart, or at all events he will be reduced to a diet of bread and water. He may have three or four boys and girls capable of well supporting the family, but dare not avail himself of such aid. Nor dare anyone employ them, the rigid, rigorous statute, called the "Elementary Education Act," not only forbidding but making it finable to do so! By the conditions of this Act all children of both sexes are required to attend school from the age of five up to fourteen, unless at an earlier period they have attained a certain standard of proficiency, fixed by the public school inspector, which will sooner release them from the obligation. This standard, however, they rarely do attain until the full time is up, the inspector not being easily satisfied; and so, during all these years, the services of the children, with the wages for such work as they might get employed at, are lost to their parents. Where these are in straitened circumstances, or absolute poverty—as too many of them are—the deprivation becomes what have called it, a grievance, as may be easily understood.

To meet this educational necessity a further condition of the Act requires each parish to provide school accommodation for all the children resident in it, and if the ordinary school or schools be not sufficient, then the inhabitants can demand the establishment of a "Board School"; that is, one controlled by a number of men elected from among the parishioners for this special purpose. Women are also eligible to be on the School-Boards, and in many places are on them.

Another reason for the establishment of Board schools is that the ordinary parish school is usually an appendage of the parish church, and so under an influence not relished by Dissenters. It is, in point of fact, subject to the almost exclusive control of the

Episcopalian [Anglican] clergyman, who can train up the children attending it in the lines of Episcopacy [Anglicanism], having them, as it were, at his mercy. Hence he is naturally opposed to the Board school, and does what he can to hinder its introduction to his parish. Failing in this, however, the thing he deems next best is to get himself elected a member of the School Board, with as many of his creed as possible, so that they may control it. For, having a majority, they can appoint the teacher—of course a zealous Episcopalian [Anglican]—and use other influences favorable to Episcopacy [Anglicanism]. True, the law does not allow sectarian religious teaching in these schools, save at certain off hours, when the children whose parents may be opposed to it are not compelled to attend. Nevertheless, infringements of this law are of common occurrence in neighborhoods where the dissenting element is weak and Episcopacy [Anglicanism] all-powerful. Besides there are other ways of inducting the latter, as it were surreptitiously. The schoolmaster will have musical talents, with a fine voice, has probably got his appointment through these, and will most likely be leader of the church choir, while the children are easily induced to join, even when those of Dissenters. Thus the thin end of the wedge is entered, and a fondness for music often terminates in conversion to the Episcopalian form of faith. It is chiefly on this account that School Board elections are contested so hotly, sometimes with an animosity bitter as between the extremes of political antagonism.

The money for maintaining Board schools comes from several sources. First there are the fees from the children attending them, for these schools are not altogether free. The poorest man has to pay twopence per week for each child he sends to them; though there are exceptional cases of extreme poverty where this is remitted. Next the Board is endowed with powers to fix and levy a rate on all the inhabitants of the parish; while as a further source of maintenance there is a Parliamentary grant from the national exchequer, the amount being in proportion to the number of children shown each year to have attended the school, conjoint with the number of their attendances. This will go far to explain why truancy is so sharply looked after; for the more scholars and attendances that can be exhibited by the register kept, the greater the Parliamentary grant to be claimed for the school. As evidence of the zeal exerted in compelling attendance I lay before the readers of THE TRIBUNE the reports of two Petty Sessions meetings, at which "school cases" were adjudicated. They are taken from *The Hereford Times*, a newspaper of the western shires, and, as will be seen, refer to the Petty Sessions of two distinct places, Ross and Tredegar. Ross is a small town of about 4,000 inhabitants; Tredegar but little larger; and it is to be observed that the reports relate to only one sitting of magistrates at each place, which occurs every fortnight. I admit the number of cases adjudicated on to be above the usual average; but there is no magistrates' meeting without one or more of them; and taking it all over the land there must be many thousands weekly:

ROSS—SCHOOL CASES.

William Loughman, engine driver, appeared on an adjourned summons charging him with neglecting to send his three children to school. An attendance order was applied for in the case of the eldest child, on the ground that he was not under proper control, the father being away from home all day, and the boy choosing to play truant in his absence.

The Bench adjudged the defendant to pay 5s. reduced costs, and made an order for the children's attendance at school.

Joseph Llewellyn Jordan, of Ross, was summoned for not sending his child to school. The case had been adjourned at the last court in the absence of the father.

The Bench made an order for the child's attendance the payment of 5s. costs.

Henry Wheeler, of Ross, whose case had been adjourned for the production of a medical certificate, was ordered to pay a fine of 5s., the

SCHOOL PERSECUTION

certificate produced referring to the illness of the child prior to the offence complained of.

A similar order was made upon William Wilson, of Ross (who did not appear), for payment of 5s. and to send the children to school.

In the cases of George Henry Hoare and William Coleman, both of Ross, orders were made in the absence of the defendants to send their children to school and to pay 5s. costs each.

The following new cases were brought before the Bench:

Mary Jarvis, Ross, one child. Fined 5s.

Ann Healey, charwoman, Ross, one child. It appeared that the father of the child had deserted his wife, and therefore a fresh summons was ordered to be served upon the father.

Thomas Cawthorne, carpenter, Walford, one child. Fined 5s.

Alfred Hodges, laborer, Walford, one child. Fined 5s.

Henry Evans, laborer, Ruardean, one child. Fined 5s.

George Mason, mason, Ruardean, one child. Adjourned to prove the efficiency of the private school to which the child is sent.

William Bailey, laborer, Ruardean, one child. Fined 5s.

Henry Carpenter, laborer, Sollershope, three children. Dismissed with a caution, and advised to apply to the Guardians for a remission of fees.

Elizabeth Lewis, charwoman, Sollershope, one child. Fined 5s.

Thomas Roberts, laborer, Upton Bishop, one child. Fined 5s.

William Whittington, laborer, Upton Bishop, one child. Fined 5s.

TREDEGAR—SCHOOL CASES

Sixty-one persons were called upon to answer for the shortcomings of their children in the matter of going to school. The prosecution was conducted by Mr. Dauncey. There were seventeen cases from Ebbw Vale, three from Rhymney and forty-one from Tredegar. The excuses put forward by the parents were various. Measles and other sickness had prevented many from attending school. One mother had rheumatic in the head, and could not do without her girl at home. A father was engaged in work and only himself earning money for the support of a wife and six children, all under ten.

One defendant asked the Bench what was to be done if he could not pay the fine?

Dr. Coates—Your goods will be distrained on, and if you have none they will take your poor body.

Defendant—Then what is to be done?

Mr. Hughes—Send your children to school.

Dr. Coates—And they will be kept out of mischief and be taught the Ten Commandments.

Mr. Hughes—I beg your pardon, they do not learn the Commandments.

Mr. Dauncey—Perhaps if you were on the Board it might be done.

Mr. Hughes—Oh no. I creased my connection with the Board on that very account.

Some of the defendants gave satisfactory reasons for the non-attendance, and such cases were adjourned. In all other cases a fine of 5s. was imposed, excepting one, in which the son had been sent to a reformatory school since the issuing of the summons.

The five-shilling fine inflicted in most of the above cases is not the full amount of damage sustained by the individuals so mulcted. In addition there is the loss of time attending the place of trail, with journeyings to and fro, —at least a day, —worth a wage of two shillings, or half a crown; and where it ends in distraint of goods, the costs will mount up to as much more. If it take not the man's "poor body," as the magistrate quaintly phrases it, it will take from him a whole week of his earnings at one fell swoop. And all this to be gone over again should the truancy be repeated.

I will make no comment on the flippant, almost unfeeling, remarks of these Tredegar Solons, as they speak volumes for themselves. But Mr. Hughes's reason for defecting from the School Board is worthy a word of explanation, since it points to the religious teaching already referred to, letting a flood of light upon it. Mr. Hughes is, of course, an Episcopalian [Anglican] clergyman, no other sort having seats upon the magisterial bench; and his objection to the Board schools is not because of their failing to teach the Ten Commandments, but leaving out other instruction of a yet more sectarian kind guiding to Episcopacy

[Anglicanism]. What he would have the children taught is that usually taught them in the good old parish schools under clerical supervision, described by a witty lady of my acquaintance as being two distinct branches of education, and only two—"the Church Catechism and their duty to their betters."

The Elementary Education Act, which brought about the establishment of Board schools, was a concession to Liberalism and well meant. But instead of a blessing it has proved more of a curse, leading to ceaseless prosecution of the poor people, or persecution of them, as it may be justly and appropriately termed. And what do their children get in return for all this harrying? Instruction that extends to the three R's—this and nothing more!

Cricket player; from A. G. Steel and Hon. L. G. Lyttleton, *Cricket* (London: Longmans Green and Co., 1888).

XIX.
The Sports of the People.

Original publication date: August 6, 1882.

Having given account of the rural sports of England's aristocracy, I devote this letter to those more peculiar to her common people—if sports they can be said to have. Certes, the list is not a long one; and as regards the lowest or laboring classes, well nigh non-existent. With them it is literally all work and no play; the time they are occupied at the former leaving them little or none for indulging in the latter. A man who has been toiling from 6 a.m. till 6 p.m. with possibly a couple of miles' walk to and from this work, is neither in the humor or condition to enjoy sport—especially if it be of the outdoor kind, and calling for physical exertion. And as his toil extend to at least 300 days in the year,—more the pity for him if it do not,—it may be inferred that his opportunities of recreation are few. IT would be his misfortune were they numerous; for if idle beyond the fifty-two Sundays and some five or six holidays allowed him, he would have the wolf drawing up to his door. With him a suspension of work means stoppage of pay; and non-employment for only one day in the week would reduce his hebdomadal wage of twelve shillings to ten, with consequent and per contra increase of his difficulty in making ends meet.

In one of my earlier letters, relating to the farm laborer, I stated his weekly wage to be scant twelve shillings, when employed permanently or by the year. As my statement has been called in question by several English newspapers devoted to the farming interest,—*The Mark Lane Express* at their head,—I may here be permitted to interpolate proof of its correctness. They who questioned it were mostly farmers, who, by a strange misconception, supposed by statistics to reflect adversely upon themselves, though I said that they had nothing to do with the lowness of labor remuneration. For the most part writing anonymously, and led by the "Man of Mark Lane," their line of argument consisted solely of allegations tending to show that these are exceptional cases of skilled laborers, who by hook, and by crook contrive to earn something more than twelve shillings a week. To this same tune sang they all, in exalted chorus; merely affirming what I myself admitted, as everyone who has read my letter must know. Some of them have set forth tables of labor statistics, ludicrously incorrect, to which I have given rejoinder and rebuttal. Luckily for these farmers, their laborers cannot scribble letters to the newspapers; if they could, the publish would be told a very different tale.

The correspondence on this subject is too long for publication in THE TRIBUNE; but, by good fortune I can substantiate my statements without that. As it chances, an eminent Queen's Counsel and County Court Judge—B. T. Williams, esq.—has just written a letter to *The London Times*; which, though relating to a different question, incidentally more than confirms me. His special purpose was to point out the iniquity of imprisonment for debt; which the outside world believes to have been long ago abolished in England. Theoretically it is so, but practically the punishment still exists—very practically, as will be seen by the extracts from Mr. Williams's letter which I lay before your readers. He says:

One half of the world has no notion how the other half fares. In the midst of our national prosperity there is suffering that finds no expression in Parliament or the Press. A return, called Mr. Norwood's return, has just been issued, which tells a story of domestic disaster in many a humble home. It appears from this return that in the year 1881 there were sent to jail, by the county court judges of England and Wales, 5,444 persons for non-payment of debts. Those who have any knowledge of the working populations of this country—of their precarious employment and mode of life, and of their large families—may appreciate to some extent the suffering which the imprisonment of so many breadwinners must have caused in their ranks. "He threatened, sir" said a good woman in my presence recently, "to send my husband to jail, but I thought that too dreadful for anyone to do, for what would have become of me and my seven young children, all dependent upon him?" The old notice that indebtedness is somewhat tainted with crime still lingers in the minds of many. It may be taken that nearly all persons summoned have no visible property that could be seized in execution. Usually they have no means of support except their wages, which are often precarious and uncertain, even in the most busy districts…We often hear of high wages in mining and manufacturing districts, and they are sometimes undoubtedly high. But advances in wages are often sudden and short, and are to be set of against long seasons of depression and poverty. An observant workingman, who had long lived in a thriving colliery district, recently told me that his estimate was that, with bad times, sickness, accidents and strikes, no working collier made, through this term of capacity for work, more than ten shillings a week for the support of himself and family. Many cherish optimist views with regard to the lives of their poor neighbors…It is no exaggeration to say that in some districts the chains of an actual slavery are around many a workingman. Imprisonment for debt, under the pretence of contumacy to the court, still exists for the working classes, and substantially only for them…It is said the working classes have the benefit of credit given them, because their creditors have the power of taking proceedings to send them to jail. But it is a credit for which enormous interest is paid, in time and money, and a credit that brings at last hopeless trouble and slavery to all who receive it. It is also to be remembered that the men sent to jail are the breadwinners of families, and that their imprisonment not only results in their becoming themselves burdens on the public, but also in throwing their wives and children upon the rates and public charity. Their clothes and goods are sold for immediate necessaries, they are obliged to incur new debts, and when the workers come out of jail, before they can again make any efforts to retrieve the misfortunes of the past, they are harassed with new orders and commitments. The evil is increasing and some day a remedy must be found for it.

In thus largely extracting from this remarkable letter, I need not remind the American reader that in England a county court judge is a man whose words are of weight, and not likely to be spoken either loosely or thoughtlessly. Nor need I point out that the wages of the workingmen Mr. Williams refers to—those of the mining and manufacturing districts—are always higher than what farm laborers receive; their work being harder, to say nothing of the risk of life. If, then, the former get only ten shillings a week, surely my statement of the latter receiving only twelve shillings is confirmed, *a tortiori*.

Returning to the sports of England's people, I repeat that the list is not a long one; and still shorter, if by the people is meant the masses of her workingmen—the true proletariat. But taking it to include the lower middle classes, the number of their recreative games and pastimes is still exceedingly limited, as also the number of those who take part in them.

Cricket stands at their head, and is regarded as a national game; almost every parish or village having its cricket club. Still, notwithstanding the noise made about it, it is not played by any considerable number of individuals; that is, in proportion to the whole people. The laboring poor have nothing to do with it, and little more have workingmen of any kind. After the fatigues of the day it is too trying; besides being attended with some expense. A cricket-ground must be kept up, and rent paid for it, though it be only a bit of meadow or pasture land. And there is yet another bar against the rural laborer's engaging in it. In hay-time and harvest, during the evening hours when he might be supposed to play it, instead of being in the cricket-field, necessity keeps him in another field of quite a different kind, slaving away to earn the few shillings extra wage of which so much has been said and made by those who give him work. Throughout spring and summer, too, in his off h ours he is equally employed at one industry or another; generally in the cultivation of his cottage garden, to eke out a trifle for household maintenance. Nor do these remarks apply only to the older men—the heads of families. They are alike applicable to the younger ones, or a large number of them; most of whom have some odd job, which keeps them toiling on as long as daylight lasts. Those not so occupied are the lazy ones, who care less for cricket than to be loitering about some beer-house, or sitting in the taproom of a cross-roads tavern.

The cricket-players are of a class socially above that of the workingmen, being chiefly young farmers; and if a club is contiguous or contingent to a town, they will be bank clerks, shopmen, the sons of tradesmen, and the more sprightly of young mechanics. Sometimes there will be a sprinkling of the *jeunesse douce* among them, the necessities of the game leading to this condescension. For cricket to be played at its best, must be "double-wicket"; which requires two "elevens," or twenty-two players; a greater number than of young gentlemen, *pur sang*, is likely to found in most neighborhoods. In remote rural parishes, thinly populated, such mixed clubs are common enough; for there the laboring man is necessarily admitted, since a match could not be made up without him. Elsewhere and otherwise, he is not wanted and will be excluded, no matter what his ambition to display skill as a batter and bowler.

However aristocratic the composition of an English country cricket club, it may surprise the American reader to learn that it is not above begging. Every year the hat is sent round, in the shape of a circular soliciting contributions for its support. Annually I myself receive such; only to fling them into the fire, with a feeling of contempt for the meanness that inspires the paltry appeal. With a multitude of poor men and their families around, many of them at starvation's door, it were a mockery of charity—indeed almost inhumanity—to devote one's dole of almsgiving to the maintenance of an idle sport. I may add, however, that in England cricket is not altogether an idle sport; but one practiced for profit, and with zealous determination to obtain it. In many cases it is a pure game of gambling, just as with the turf, the dice-box and the card-table.

In most parts of the country, after cricket, football may be said to have second place; a game more played by the poorer classes, chiefly because of its being expensive. There is only the cost of the ball itself, a matter of three or four shillings, and this shared among several amounts to little or nothing. And as an ordinary pasture field is all that is required for the play, there is usually some generous land-owner or occupier who gives this gratis. Still, for the laboring man, football has many of the drawbacks I have shown as belonging to cricket. It calls for an output of bodily exertion he is not disposed to make, after having done his day's work; moreover, the daylight may be gone before this is done, leaving him no time for kicking a football. Withal, there are many of the younger men—strong and vigorous they must be—who do kick it, up to a late hour of the night, when there chances to be a moon! And, nor unfrequently, kick one another's shins, or come in violent collision, to their serious detriment, even with fatal results. So many such have of late occurred that there have been newspaper protests and outcry against this rough, unaristocratic game.

Of the few other summer and out-door diversions of the English rustic, quoits may be mentioned, though it is a game rather rare and exceptional. So also "nip-cat-and-run," with several similar contrivances of a trifling kind, and more or less local. "Pitch-and-toss" is played; but this being against the law has to be carried on surreptitiously, under cover of a hedge, or in the heart of a wood. English country boys still play at marbles, as did their predecessors of a century ago; and I regret to add, cheat at them with undiminished audacity.

Few as are the summer sports of England's poorer people, still fewer have they in winter—indeed scarce any. There is skating when the ice is strong enough to bear; a thing of so rare occurrence

THE SPORTS OF THE PEOPLE

that there are winters—as the last, for instance—with scarce any ice at all. Besides, skating is not a pastime of the lower classes; nor was it one of the middle until a very modern date. Ten years ago no one thought of practising it, save the scions of aristocracy, young gentlemen and ladies. Then, around the frozen lakes or ponds on which these disported themselves, the lower social world stood in wondering gaze to witness their graceful gliding and cutting figures of 8. But the severe winters of 1879-'80 and 1880-'81 brought about a change, and the sport was no longer exclusive. A skating mania set in, and every sheet of ice became crowded by skaters of both sexes, and all ranks of society. No, not all; the poor proletarian, being here again excluded; partly because he could not afford to pay for a pair of skates, and partly that his wearing them would be deemed the height of presumption. Sufficient enjoyment for him is a slide; at least such is the opinion of his superiors, whatever he may think himself. And to sliding he resorts, having little or no alternative sport during the chill winter days. But a rueful sport it is, should he be the father of a family. For the frost enabling him to indulge in it will have also thrown him out of work; and while scoring the ice with his heavy hob-nailed shoes he may be thinking of his wife at home shivering over a fireless hearth, and his children clamoring for bread.

Apart from the pastimes of the nature of games, in rural England there are amusements of an associate kind, partaken of by the people *en masse*. Such are school entertainments, club-festivals, holiday fetes, harvest-homes and the like; account of which must needs be reserved for another letter.

The Harvest Home; from *Finden's Tableaux*, 1841.

XX.
Associate Pastimes.

Original publication date: August 13, 1882.

Of associate diversions which vary the rural life of England the "Harvest-Home" may be taken as a type. This festival, old as agriculture itself, is still observed in most parts of the kingdom, and with a ceremony equalling that of ancient days. The clergy lend countenance to and invest it with something of a semi-religious character; a service in the church being one of its accompaniments. By the clergy and church I, of course, mean the Episcopalian [Anglican], as "Harvest-Homes" are chiefly under their patronage, even in districts where Dissenters form a large element of the population. The non-conformist ministers may preach a harvest of "thanksgiving sermon," but this is a Sunday affair and quite apart from the festival itself, which is celebrated with sports of a class the strict Non-conformist does not approve of. With him it is a relic of the old objection to dangerous frivolities urged by his ancestors in the time of the first Charles, and which Charles commanded practice of—even on the Lord's Day. For this reason the Harvest-Home is generally, though tacitly, understood as having affiliation with the State Church; and the incumbent of the parish, be he rector or vicar, is expected to figure at it; which he rarely fails to do, the duty being pleasant, as popular. As the name implies, it takes place after harvest, when the cereal crops have been garnered, and, as already said, there is service in the church, the clergyman preaching an appropriate sermon. The sacred edifice will be decorated for the occasion; not with evergreens, as at Christmas, but bunches of wheat, barley and other symbols of Ceres, also flowers, all more or less elegantly arranged according to the taste and talents of the young ladies who do the decoration.

The religious part of the performance over, there is adjournment to some neighboring field or meadow suitable for the sports to follow. These are of various kinds, mostly of an athletic character, and somewhat differing in different districts of the country. The usual list includes football, and quoits, with foot races, both "flat" and over hurdles. There will be "running in sacks" too; that is the runners tied up in corn sacks, legs, arms and everything, with only the head left out; these comical competitors by their contortions and tumbles eliciting peals of laughter. Aged men are sometimes pitted against one another in foot races, the prize being so much tobacco; and even old women occasionally thus contend, a pound of tea or a piece of printed calico, sufficient for a gown, rewarding the winner. Jumping—the "broad" jump and the "long"—is left to more youthful athletes; as also "climbing the greased pole," this last, from its difficulty and the many failures attendant, affording much amusement to the spectators. But there is an encouragement to success; he who first performs the feat of censorial agility becoming entitled to a leg of pork, shoulder or mutton, or some such emolument. "Kiss in the ring" is another diversion of the Harvest-Home; a more gentle one, and to the young rustics of both sexes perhaps pleasanter. With some at all events it is highly popular.

Around the arena of the sports will be seen a number of hucksters, seated or standing behind their stalls erected for the occasion. They have come from the neighboring towns or village, bringing their commodities with them, which consist of nuts, fruits, cakes and other kinds of confectionary. These thrifty traffickers often do a profitable stroke of business at Harvest-Homes, when the gathering chances to be a large one. So also do the purveyors of shooting galleries, and those who set up "Aunt Sally" to be knocked down for a cocoanut. Commonly a conspicuous feature of the field is a large tent or marquee in which drink is retailed, beer, cider, wines, with sometimes spirits, as brandy and whiskey. The

ASSOCIATE PASTIMES

caterer of these is the keeper of some near public-house, who has erected the tent by leave of him who owns the field. But for the sale of spirits in this way he needs other permission, that of the district magistrates, and this refused, as it often is, and should be, only ginger beer, lemonade and the like non-intoxicating beverages are to be got upon the ground. When it is thus, there will be much going and coming between the roadside taverns and the place of sports.

As the shades of evening begin to darken the out-door diversions are brought to an end and there is a second adjournment this time to the school house. The desks and benches have been cleared away and the room made ready for dancing, which will be carried on till the hour of midnight. The band that has been performing all the day furnishes the music of the night. In many these rustic dances may be noted a social commingling rarely or never seen elsewhere; fashionable ladies, as the rector's and squire's daughters, footing it with young farmers or even a sprightly laborer, having for partners men whom if met next morning they would scarce deign to acknowledge by a nod. English country life shows some queer eccentricities; and when "society" thus mixes with the people it is pure condescension, the motive not always a noble one. Withal, admission to the dancing is not free, entrance within the school-room requiring to be paid for—usually sixpence. The refreshments are tea, with bread and butter, the charge for a cup of the former and slice of the latter being threepence. Formerly on the occasion of "Harvest-Home" the farmers in most parishes were accustomed to give their laborers a half-holiday, as also defray the expenses of the entertainment. There is little or nothing of that now, agricultural depression account for the change; and a laborer who takes the half-holiday will have his day's wages docked in proportion. To him, therefore, Harvest-Homes are no longer as joyous or congenial as they used to be; and likely the coming autumn will see them at a still lower ebb of joviality.

Of a kindred nature to the Harvest-Home, though in many respects different, is the "Cottage-garden show." It is of less common occurrence, and altogether a quieter affair, with no sports attendant, the show itself being considered sufficient attraction. This consists of various garden products—vegetables, roots, fruits and flowers—set out on tables for exhibition, under a large awning or tent. Each article is labeled with the name of the cultivator, especially those that have taken prizes; for it is a prize competition, with the object of encouraging horticulture among the laboring poor.

Promoted by the clergy and resident gentry of the neighborhood the cottage-garden show is generally held in private grounds, as on the law of the rectory or vicarage; and all classes are admitted to it free. Still there is a line of demarcation between the tent where the articles are on exhibition, and the bit of better-kept ground nearer the house occupied by the *elite*. Within this inner circle tabooed to the common people, be they exhibitors or not, tables are also set out, but not for show; the things on them being eatables and drinkables for immediate consumption. They will show an array of sweet-cakes, grapes, melons and other fruits of the orchard and hothouse, with decanters of sherry and pitchers of claret and champagne-cup. At intervals groups of ladies and gentlemen approach this al fresco spread, eat a bit of sponge or other cake, sip a glass of wine, and saunter off again; possibly not half of them paying a visit to the exhibition tent, or thinking of aught that is in it. To them the cottage-garden show is just like an ordinary "garden-party"—with the lawn-tennis and archery eliminated. What the poor people think on such occasions were matter for speculation and conjecture; but it has often occurred to me that their thoughts cannot be of the happiest—even with those who have won rewards for their industry. Looking across that forbidden boundary—which may be but an imaginary line, still well understood as saying: "Thus far shalt thou come and no farther"—toeing the mark, as it were, and seeing their so-called

ASSOCIATE PASTIMES

"betters" quaffing, and delightedly laughing—it were difficult to believe that they can be alike delighted. For in this exhibition, ostensibly meant for their benefit, they behold a spectacle more calculated to make them feel humiliation reminding them, and with unblushing plainness, of the wide gulf which yawns between their class and the superiors of society.

Cottage garden-shows are not much affected by farmers, or people in the middle ranks of life. Nor are many such present at them; indeed scarce any and for obvious reasons. Were they to attend, their place would be among the poor cottagers, per chance their own laborers, in and around the show tent. It would be deemed presumption on their part to enter the sacred precinct where those called *their* betters also, have exclusive possession. Hence, natural, and no wonder, their repugnance to appearing in an assemblage so invidiously assorted.

The gathering at a cottage-garden show dissolves at an early hour; not breaking up *en masse* but gradually melting away. On the roads leading from it may be seen the exhibitors going homeward in groups, afoot of course, and bearing back the products exhibited; some of them, the unsuccessful ones, rather down in the mouth, while the prize-winners will be highly jubilant. For they have a pleasant expectation of something beyond the prize already gained—sale of seed from the commodity that has won it, at a fancy price. These exhilarated ones may feel less envious of the "carriage fold," also on return home, now and then whirled past them; and less disposed to be angry at the dust from wheels flung back in their faces.

Another kind of rural entertainment much in vogue and which may be mentioned next in order, is the "School-Treat." It is a tea given to the children who attend the parish school, including the age poor of both sexes. To all these it is free; the cost being defrayed by voluntary contribution from the wealthier parishioners. It takes place in the school-room, the children coming thither provided with their own cups or mugs; for, otherwise to get together such an array of crockery were a somewhat difficult matter. The tea brewed in kettles and thence transferred to large jugs, is carried around and poured into the cups; bread and butter, with cakes, being the accompaniment. Sometimes oranges are also distributed among the delighted juveniles. The officiating waitresses are the young ladies of the parish, led by the parson; and young gentlemen occasionally appear among them to make the duty pleasanter, if not lighter. At these festivals where the extremes of youth and old age come into juxtaposition there will be amusements of a suitable kind; outdoor sports if in summer; and in winter displays of the magic lantern with recitations and songs accompanied by the piano. They have rarely anything to do with school examinations; being got up more for the enjoyment of the children, and perhaps a little by way of pastime to the fashionable patronesses of the entertainment. Another motive may be added—to make the school popular, and so draw students.

The school treat, however, is not exclusive to schools connected with the parish, or Episcopalian [Anglican] church. Dissenters have them as well, and often in grand degree; sectarian zeal rallying strong to their support. The members of a Nonconformist chapel—be it Baptist, Methodist or Congregational—contribute generously to the school treat, either in cash or the materials of the feast—tea, sugar, bread, butter and home-baked cakes.

With the Dissenting people, and almost special to them, is another and kindred form of entertainment—the "Tea-meeting," *pur sang*. It is usually semi-annual, one in summer and one in winter; on each occasion attracting a large assemblage. When in summer the spread will be out of doors in some picturesque spot chosen by the managing committee—a sort of monster picnic. There will be an admonishing address by the minister who presides, with hymns sung. Sports also are permitted, but of a more gentle nature than the rough athletic games of the Harvest-Home. For the minister sets his face against such high jinks, above all against dancing. Still "kiss in the ring" is allowable; under such supervision being deemed immaculately innocent. In winter the tea meeting is held in the chapel school-room, or where there is none, or one not large enough, in the chapel itself. Here again the minister gives a lecture of admonition, and there is hymn-singing with the modest accompaniment of a harmonium. The grand organ is not yet an appanage of many English Dissenting places of worship. These tea meetings have a purpose apart from mere amusement. By the vilest of all national laws the Nonconformist faith of England not only rests on voluntary support, but its professors have to contribute to that of a Church and creed antagonistic, and which they do not believe in. Hence every exertion is required of them to maintain existence; and so admission to the tea-meeting is not free, but must be paid for—the proceeds going toward the defrayment of chapel expenses.

I had hoped in this letter to conclude my account of associate rural pastimes; but looking forward to the long array of "Foresters' fetes," celebrations of "Odd Fellows," "Ancient Shepherds" and "Club feasts," with "School Concerts" and "Penny Readings," I must ask indulgence and space for "another of the same."

Foresters' Fete; from *The Graphic*, September 16, 1871.

XXI.
Other Associate Pastimes.

Original publication date: August 20, 1882.

England abounds in the various mutual-help associations—"Freemasonry," "Odd Fellows," Ancient Orders of "Foresters," "Shepherds," and "Druids." Of course they are not all special to England, nor yet to its country places, the towns having them as well, though in these noticeable by reason of the surroundings. In rural districts they are more conspicuous, especially at theta time of the year when they hold their "anniversaries," or "fete," as sometimes called. These take place through the summer season, each "Lodge," "Court," "Branch," or whatever the subdivision be, having its own. A dinner is the usual form of entertainment, followed by outdoor sports, and, as with the Harvest Home, preceded by a religious service in the parish church; for in most places Episcopalianism [Anglicanism] affects to take these purely secular associations under its protecting wing.

A "Foresters' fete" may be regarded as typical of all the others, though rather more demonstrative than they, and with some features additional. On the morning of the day set apart for it, the members of a particular "Court" assemble at an appointed place, dressed gala fashion, and wearing the insignia of their order. But there will be a number of them costumed unlike the rest; one as the famed archer of Sherwood forest, in tunic of Lincoln green, plumed hat, tights and russet boots; a second got up to represent Little John; a third, Will Scarlet; a fourth, Friar Tuck, with others of the outlawed band, while not unfrequently the Sheriff of Nottingham and Maid Marian figure in the picturesque group. Often these costumed characters appear on horseback, and so make the spectacle more imposing. The procession formed with a band of music at its head, they betake them to the parish church, where they are met by the clergyman, who preaches them a sermon from some appropriate text, admonishing to works of charity. After that, reforming ranks, they march around the roads; then proceed to dinner, which is usually at some roadside inn or public-house having room enough to hold them. The repast, already bespoke and provided, is of the substantial order, and plenty of it; fairly well got up, [word illegible], the landlords of such hostelries having something more than mere pride in preparing—a character to sustain, which may affect after-patronage of a similar sort. At dinner the clergyman presides, unless a still grander dignity, the Squire be present, when the latter would be expected to occupy the chair, the former being vice. Most generally, however, the parson himself performs the duties of chairman, flanked by the more distinguished of the brethren, while the vice-chair will be filled by a sprig of squiredom, or some retired officer of the Army or Navy resident in the neighborhood. There are speeches, proposing and seconding the usual round of loyal and patriotic toasts, ending with that of the day, "Prosperity to Court Black of the Ancient Order of Foresters!" Then adjournment out of doors to some field where sports and games succeed, very much the same as at Harvest Home, though often on a grander scale. Where it is a wealthy and numerous Court of the A.O.F. under big patronage, there will be a large crowd assembled; and in addition to "climbing the greased pole," with other athletes, there may be a "Morris dance" around a pole wreathed with many-colored ribbons. At night comes another adjournment indoors again, for dancing of the common kind, which will be kept up till the small hours of morning. But if the ball-room be in the inn where dinner was eaten, as it generally is, then a "special license" for its keeping open to such hours must be obtained from the magistrate. This is rarely, if ever, refused; the object being charitable, and therefore praiseworthy.

   As already said, very similar to the Foresters' fetes, though perhaps neither so picturesque nor popular, are the anniversaries of

OTHER ASSOCIATE PASTIMES

Odd Fellows, Ancient Shepherds, and Druids. And still more soberly conducted are the celebrations of the oldest order of all—the Freemasons. As most of the above-named associations, with their forms and festivals, are no doubt known in the United States, I will not further dwell upon them, but pass on to one more characteristic of rural England—the "Club Feast." It is a dinner, too, the diners being members of a club. Not a club of the fashionable world, however; instead, one chiefly composed of workingmen, some of them the poorest and lowest in the social scale. "Friendly" or "Mutual Benefit" Societies they are indifferently termed; their object being of a kindred nature with those of the Foresters or Odd Fellows. But unlike the Courts and Lodges of these, the clubs are unconnected with one another; each standing on its own basis, and acting independently. They exist all over the land, no village, nor parish, being without one or more of them, for their *raison d'etre* and necessity of existence, are everywhere keenly felt. To the English laboring-man the motives for belonging to such associations are manifold; comprising fear of want in times of continued sickness, dread of the workhouse when old age overtakes him, anxiety about the dear ones to be left behind at death, with the same for himself receiving decent burial. To guard against these dangers, and allay apprehension, he becomes a member of a Friendly Society, and contributes his share to its fund, from year to year accumulating. The whole amount rarely reaches a high figure, £300, or $1,500, being above the average. I quote this from the latest audited accounts of a club in my own neighborhood, known to be one of the most prosperous in the country. It numbers one hundred contributing members; and as out of this modest sum has to come many payments for support in cases of sickness, with funeral expenses should the sickness end in death, it needs not pointing out what a mite will remain for distribution otherwise, and how little the dead man's widow or orphans can receive. Less still—aye, sometimes nothing—where there has been default. For although the law takes cognizance of these societies—Government requiring them to be registered and to some extent to be looked after—still, now and then, a dishonest treasurer filches from their fund, or makes away with it altogether, himself going alone. The accumulation of years—often half a lifetime—thus squandered and lost, is to the poor men more than discouragement—in fact a real calamity; and to prevent the occurrence of such a bill is now before Parliament for the periodical inspection, and auditing, of Friendly Societies' accounts, by Government officials, to be appointed for this special purpose.

Discussing these dry and rather cheerless details, I return to the brighter side of the picture—the Club Feast. As with the festivals of the other combined associations above referred to, it is of annual occurrence, and like them also takes the shape of a dinner. In England there are few celebrations worthy of the name without this substantial ceremony of the stomach, deemed the *ne plus ultra* of entertainment. And by none is it more appreciated than by the members of a mutual benefit society, especially a country one, many of whom do not sit down to an orthodox dinner threescore times in the year. On nigh three hundred days of it a large proportion of them dine by the ditch side, their frugal repast consisting of bread and cold bacon, when not still more stinted, as it often is, to a "kitchen" of skim-milk cheese, or a salt herring. To these involuntary authorities the Club Feast, with its beef and mutton, roast and boiled, its apple pies and plum puddings—to say naught of beer flowing as from a free tap—is a banquet beyond anything ever enjoyed by Lucullus. To give a detailed description of the Club Feast were almost to repeat that of the other anniversary festivals. Like them it is generally regarded as a parish affair, and under patronage of the Episcopalian clergyman. There are exceptions to this, however, in districts where Dissenters form the bulk of the population. But the rule is as above; and the parish incumbent, be he rector or vicar, lends his countenance, with patronizing support, to such a club as may have been established in his parish. Usually he presides over the dinner, after having

OTHER ASSOCIATE PASTIMES

administered service in the church, with a sermon, too. And often, though not always, the dinner will come off in the school-room, a caterer providing it at so much per head—usually 3 shillings. Whether in school-room or inn there are speeches and toasts of a somewhat similar character to those already commented upon. The club's accounts are also audited and passed, with votes of thanks to the chairman and secretary. After dinner the club members, with others who have dined with them—for the feast is free to outsiders on payment of the 3 shillings—proceed to the field of sports. These are of the customary kind, though rarely on so large a scale, or so varied, as at harvest-homes and Foresters' fetes. But, as with these, there will be dancing afterward, kept up to a late hour of the night, the votaries of Terpsichore paying for admission to the ball-room, whether it be in the school-house or a public hostelry.

I had almost forgotten to mention one of the fashions of these Friendly Societies, which, however, is not all their own, but often followed by other mutual-help associations. Before sitting down to dinner the members of the club from into procession order, and, with their banner displayed, and band playing a march, they visit the houses of the wealthier inhabitants in the neighborhood, and treat them to a tune or two. This, ostensibly by way of compliment, has a very different motive, a contribution of money being expected in payment for the daylight serenade. *Nolens volens*, it is generally given; but I fancy oftener *nolens* than *volens*, and sometimes with a grimace. It is like paying the piper by those who take no part in, nor care for, the dance. Another specialty of rural diversion is the "pigeon-match" —that is, a shooting-match with pigeons as the mark. For this cruel pastime is no longer confined to the fashionable marksmen of Hurlingham and the Gun Club, but has become common all over the country. Pigeon-matches are chiefly promoted by the landlords of public houses, who advertise a fat sheep or pig to be shot for, with a cheap half-crown dinner to follow. Boniface looks for his best returns from the liquor to be sold; for although the crowd thus attracted and collected may not all dine, all are pretty sure to drink. They who attend pigeon-matches are generally the rougher elements of the population, as might be expected, and the sport (?) with its adjuncts is in every way reprehensible.

A pastime or entertainment of a more praiseworthy kind is the "school concert," or, as often called, "penny-reading," the latter name having reference to the price of admission, supposed to be a penny. The supposition, however, is not always in consonance with the fact, three pence or even six pence being oftener the scale of charge—at least to the majority of the audience. The entertainment is more special to winter; and, as may be deduced from one of its names, takes place in that hall of universal utility, the parish schoolroom. It, too, is under clerical patronage, the object being to promote intellectual enjoyment, with an eye to money proceeds; at least enough of this to cover all expenses. For music there will be a piano lent for the occasion, at which the clergyman's daughter presides, or it may be the squire's or some other young lady of the parish; and sometimes they take it in turns. The performance on the platform consists of songs and glees, with recitations, the so-called readings interspersed; and at times some musical genius of the neighborhood will delight the audience with a solo on the violin or cornet obligato. The performers of both sexes belong to every rank of life, the necessity for this social commingling being the same as that attendant on a cricket match. And when the parish itself cannot supply sufficient talent, musical or oratorical, outside aid is called in to make up the deficiency. Sometimes this has even to be paid for, certain rustic stars in the entertainment line requiring a remuneration for their services. There are concerts and readings of a purely professional kind, given in the market towns and larger villages. But the reward to the givers is not great, even in the case of those who enjoy a world-wide popularity. If I mistake not, the late Mr. Bellew, who stood at the head of popular reciters, rarely received more than £10 per night, which included his appearing upon the platform, travelling and all other expenses paid by himself! Nor is England the place to make a fortune by lecturing. The lecture, as you have it in the States, has here hardly an existence. True, there are public and professional lecturers hear of now and then in the larger provincial towns, more rarely visiting the smaller ones. But if their subjects be of a highly intellectual character, they must either go unpaid or address themselves to their audiences. The proportion of men and women in England desirous of drinking from a fount of knowledge is small compared with those who thirst for it in the United States. The reason is obvious, to me at least, and may be stated in a phrase of six words—the inspiring influence of republican institutions.

Form the sports and pastimes I have given account of, it might be supposed that the English people—even the poorest—enjoy life in a high and general degree. Yet no supposition could be more illusory or farther away from fact; and I doubt whether in all the world there be a people who know less of life's delights and more of its disagreeables than those of "merry England."

Mayne Reid would have been familiar with the Market hall at Ross-on-Wye, Herefordshire (photo taken circa 1890); courtesy Library of Congress, Washington, D.C.

XXII.
Markets, Fairs, and "Mop" Fairs.

Original publication date: August 27, 1882.

Markets figure largely in the rural life of England; for although held in towns it is country people who are chiefly concerned in them. To these they afford convenient opportunity for the disposal of farm produce, as also for purchasing articles of household need of a better quality and on better terms than can be had at the cross-roads shop. In every shire there are ten of a dozen towns privileged to hold markets—for it is a thing of license and charter—standing at an average of seven or eight miles apart. Seven is the legally prescribed minimum. In each the market is weekly; those nearest to one another holding it on different days, so that sellers and buyers may attend two or more of them, if needing or desiring it. In most of these towns every second, or alternate, market is termed a "stock market," that is, where, in addition to the lesser products of the farm, cattle, sheep and pigs are offered for sale. Horses are not regarded as a commodity of the ordinary markets; though now and then an aged pony will change hands at them, or a worn-out Rosinante, "screws" not worth sending the distant Horse Repository or reserving for the fair of rarer occurrence. Each market-town has its "market-house," centrally situated, and often a quaint, ancient structure, supported on piers. It is two stories high, the lower one open, the upper occupied by a spacious apartment known as the "Town Hall." In this, on market-days, farmers meet millers, and corn-dealers with their samples, as also the purveyors of oil-cake and other cattle foods, with theirs. In the same place they transact business with the agents of chemical manure companies, whose samples are aught but sweet-smelling.

THE RURAL LIFE OF ENGLAND

The Town Hall is the place of Petty Sessions, a raised platform at one end being the magistrates' bench. Public meetings are also held in it, with those of the Board of Guardians, and the like; while in the winter it is occasionally utilized as a concert room, or let for a night or so to some company of strolling players. Of late years, however, the more progressive towns have erected "Corn Exchanges,"—buildings of simple accommodations and more attractive,—so that many of the above-named assemblages have forsaken the antiquated Town Hall for these. Still the old market-house remains the place of petty traffic; and on market days, in its open under-story and the space adjacent, will be seen an agglomeration of stalls loaded with butter, eggs, dressed poultry, fish, fruit and vegetables, served by hucksters of both sexes, through chiefly of the fair. There will be a display of fresh meat, also,—beef, mutton and pork,—which some speculative country butcher has brought thither, not to the delight of those of the town, who deem it somewhat of an intrusion upon their domain. But as the rural knight of the knife and steel has paid the market's toll, he is entitled to a stand in it, and they cannot hinder his competition.

In the open market-place, or a wide street leading from it, will be a row of little carts with the horses out of them, but the lading still on. This consists of live poultry in all its varieties,—geese, ducks, turkeys and barn-door fowls, —carried in hampers, crates, or under netting, to prevent escapes. A noisy quarter it is; for in addition to the cacklings, with now then the resonant crow of a chanticleer, some displeased henwife may be heard in loud dispute with the "fowl-badger," as the wholesale poultry dealer is called. A rough and often foul-mouthed fellow he; though no unfrequently a sturdy country woman of the cottager class, with a basket of chickens slung over her robust, brawny arm., will give him his change in full, as in kind. When a sale comes off the fracas reaches its height; a deafening din, as the two-legged live stock is transferred from crate to crate and cart to cart.

In and around the market-house are many other noises; for not all the hucksters sit silent behind their stalls. Some stand up, as the hawker of cheap fish,—usually asseverating the freshness of his haddocks, herrings and mackerel. Often the sanitary inspector holds a different opinion about this; with result that the purveyor of brain phosphorous gets "pulled up," and fined for selling food unit for human use. The dealer in china and crockery is also one of the noisy ones. He stands in the midst of his wares,—a grand spread of them exposed on the pavement,—with a dining plate in each hand, or it may be a couple of jugs; and while setting forth their superior quality, gives proof of it by bringing them together with a crash and concussion, seemingly violent enough to shatter both. Yet no breakage occurs, not so much as a crack! How the thing is done I have not the slightest idea, though often seeing it done. The ceramic puzzle, however, well answers the salesman's purpose; as the farmers' and cottagers' wives, with sad experience of the frailty of crockeryware, step up and purchase his unbreakable plates, mugs and jugs without further hesitation.

Now and then the vendor of a patent medicine appears in the market-place, with glib tongue vaunting the virtues of his cure-all or heal-all. He sits on the box of a four-wheeled vehicle, or the dogcart or commercial traveller's "trap" kind, covered in, and filled with bottles of the stuff. Nor does he vaunt it in vain, but with sure success; bottle after bottle being sold, often till the trap is empty. Many of the rustics, men as well as women, who buy his patent medicine, have not the remotest idea of what it is meant for, beyond his own *ipse dixit*. They swallow it all the same, soon as they get home, and fancy it does them good. Likely it does them no great harm; since in several judicial trials on the ingredients of such mixtures proved on analysis to be harmless enough, though sufficiently disgusting to have produced sickness themselves.

In the market-house, on market-days, auction sales of furniture are occasionally held; old and of an inferior quality, but comprising all sorts of odds and ends, from a damaged door-mat to a four-post mahogany bedstead. At these sales "bargains" are frequently picked up by the poorer class of farmers or their wives, to be taken back home with them in their "market-traps." The still poorer laborers also avail themselves of such opportunities, the chattels they buy being carried to their cottage homes on a donkey cart; it may be upon their own backs or in their hands. Still another exhibit of the markets is an array of agricultural implements; these brand-new, and of all the kinds popular and approved of, with others seeking approval. If glaring colors could give it, none of them need be deemed undeserving, since all appear in the gaudiest of red and the brightest of blue, each labelled with the manufacturer's name and address. Most of these manifold implements of machines are as nearly perfect as may be; and an American inspecting them would find that those nearest perfection are the product of his own country, from the ponderous steam plough or horse reaper to the lightest and tiniest of hay pikes. This may seem strange, though there is nothing strange in it, but simply the natural outcome of republican institutions—of mind and brain left free to conceive and invent, instead of being trammeled and obstructed by the many petty antagonistic influences met with in all countries cursed by monarchical rule. The imperfection of the English patent laws forms an influential factor against invention, not only from the cost of taking out a patent, but the slight protection it affords when taken out. In England any number of people may patent the same article without regard to the principle involved, or its specifications, and the Patent Office will take the money from all,—£200 each when complete,—leaving them afterward to fight it out among themselves.

The space set apart for the exhibition of these agricultural implements, as of everything else, has to be paid for. No stand or stall can escape the "market-toll," nor is traffic allowed anywhere in the streets without it. Even the poor cottager's wife, with her basket of boarded hen's eggs—be it but a couple of dozen—must submit to this municipal mulct, to her a very blackmail in seeming, as it is in reality. It may take only a penny or "tuppence," still it makes a big hole in the three or four sixpences she expects to get for the contents of her little basket. She can only avoid it by direct sale to the consumer at his own house. And she must needs be a known and old customer; else many a door-bell may be rung in vain, and many a denial given by saucy housemaid, saying: "No! we don't want any of your eggs"; with a probability of the door being banged to in the poor woman's face.

The stock market is held in a different place from all the above; generally outside the town, or in a thinly inhabited suburb. Its insignia are a one-storied shed-like building, for shelter, should it rain; and contiguous to or surrounding it, a large space inclosed by iron hurdles. A portion of this inclosure is further subdivided into pens for sheep and pigs, the remainder left open for the cattle. Most of all sorts are disposed of by auction, the local auctioneers or any others having the carriage of sale. The commission charged is at the usual rate, 5 per cent, or a "shilling in the pound." This does not include the market-toll, which must be paid on every animal that enters the inclosure, whether sold by auction of private sale, and whether sold or not. The sheep are disposed of first, because likeliest to suffer by prolonged absence from their partners; after them the pigs; and lastly the cattle. Among these fat beeves for the butcher will be in the majority, and young stock to be kept over. Milch cows are also brought to market, but rarely one without a calf at foot, and often not her own calf, though represented as being so. The creature she gave birth six or eight weeks before—since fatted and killed—may at the moment be hanging up in some butcher's shop; while the "staggering Bob," floundering and bawling by her side, is but a foster calf, which till that morning or the evening before has never drawn milk from her teats. But why all this? the innocents may ask. Simply to make believe that the cow has but lately calved, and so is more valuable from having all her milk yet to come. Her largely distended udder will be confirmatory of this belief to those ignorant of the fact that she has not been milked either on that day or the preceding. The morality, or rather immorality, of this transaction does not very forcibly affect the ordinary English cattle-dealer; and, I am sorry to add, many farmers make light of it; some having been even know to boast "how neatly they did the trick."

At the stock-market held just before Christmas there is always an unusually large offering of fat cattle; roast beef being a universal viand of the English Christmas Day dinner. On that day the poorest people make an effort to have a joint of it on their tables, and the butchers view with one another in showing a well-filled shop; the meat, beef or mutton, systematically arranged upon their stalls, and festooned over with evergreens. Prize cups, silver or plated, are awarded to those who bring the fattest and best beeves to this market; the donors being either auctioneers who have the sale of them, or the purveyors of cattle-foods and condiments, each by way of advertising his own special commodity, and so obtaining other customers for it. All of these odd doings are duly chronicled in the local papers, where two or three columns will be devoted to a description of the butchers' shops, with details of how they are decorated; the animals slaughtered and hanging up in them, with their weight, condition, price and pedigree, not omitting who bred and fed each and every [one] of them. For it is a feather in the butcher's cap to have it know that his beef has been browsed on the pasture of some county magnate—all the better if a titled one,—and his mutton fatted by some noted flock-master.

About the same time, close preceding Christmas, there occurs another specialty of market, known as the "big poultry market," also a provider for the Christmas festivities. It is held either in the Town Hall or Corn Exchange, over the floor of which stand tables arranged in rows, but apart as in a restaurant, each groaning under a load of turkeys, geese, ducks and barn-door fowls; dead , of course, and dressed in the most attractive styles. Presiding over the tables are middle-aged dames in their Sunday attire, with many younger ones got up "in grand fig"; if not in the first fashion of young ladies, very near to it. They are the wives and daughters of farmers, even big farmers, who on this particular anniversary condescend to play the part of hucksters. Most of them have a "pin-money" interest in the proceeds of sale, and so do their best to obtain high prices. The gentry of the neighborhood visit the "big poultry show," as it is also called, and perambulate around the tables, inspect, select and purchase such bird or birds as may seem most suitable, with price taken into account. They are sold either by weight or by "hand,"—that is, at so much a head; the finest turkeys fetching twenty-five shillings, or ever $5, each. The price, however, is a good deal dependent on the time of day, with the demand. In the morning hours, up till 12 or 1, the fair saleswomen carry their heads high, and ask full value, if not considerably more. Later on in the afternoon, should much of the stock remain on hand, threatening an unsold surplus, their flag becomes lowered, and "bargains" may be obtained from them. Then is the opportunity for the economic householder, who, knowing, takes advantage of it, slips in, and buys a turkey for ten shillings, which a few hours earlier would have been refused him at twenty! For it would never do to take the dead poultry back home again, and not much better would be the only other alternative—selling at wholesale to the "fowl-badgers."

The English fair is only a market on a more extended scale, and with some extra characteristics. It is, of course, of less frequent occurrence, in most towns held only semi-annually, though in some quarterly. And there is distinction between fairs as regards popularity, with the articles bought and sold at them; some having a celebrity as horse fairs, other being more noted for horned cattle, and still others where sheep or pigs are the specialty. In all cases, however, there is much resemblance between one and the other— and unmistakable idiosyncrasy which bespeaks it to be a *fair*. For whatever the substantial commodities there exhibited, at each and all will be encountered a complete exhibition of frivolities and amusements so attractive to the rustic mind. A wide street or suburban road, for the length of a half mile or more, will be crowded with tents, booths, covered vans and caravans, their occupants being proprietors of wax-works and wild beast menageries, with giants, giantesses and dwarfs—in short, the whole fraternity of traveling showmen. Likely a company of strolling players, too, who can perform the grandest tragedies— "Macbeth," or "Richard the Third,"—on a stage six feet by ten. "Aunt Sallies" and "shooting galleries" take up a portion of the space; while here and there a bawling ballad-singer or a "cheap jack" auctioneer makes the surrounding noisy. The thimble-riggers and performers of card tricks do their work in a quieter way, now then looking furtively around to make sure there is no policeman near. Still more watchful and wary of him in the blue tunic and black helmet are the pickpockets, who muster at every fair plentiful as mice in a rickyard. Nor can one proceed far without meeting some of the Romany folk, gypsies of every age and both sexes. Here an old withered hag with face as wrinkled parchment accosts you; there it will be young girl, whose chief claim to good looks lies in a certain picturesqueness of features and attire. In either case the salutation will be the same, "Pretty gentleman!" (or "beautiful lady" if it be one of the fair sex who is solicited) "Won't you let me tell your fortune? I'll do it for a silver sixpence." The flattering words rarely fail to have effect, either on the "pretty gentleman" or the "beautiful lady"; and the silver sixpence is dropped into the gypsy's outstretched palm, without care whether the fortune be forecast or not. The number of nomad and vagabond people of all the above sorts who attend English fairs, going from one to the other, and making it their sole occupation or resource, must be enormous.

Something different from the ordinary fairs are the "mop" or "hiring" fairs; which in England are not yet extinct, but flourish in many parts of the country. At these a spectacle is presented, ancient in kind, but which, would no doubt be new to most

Americans. For they would there see mean and women of every age, though the majority of them youthful,—boys and girls,—standing in rows, or groups, as on inspection, as they really are. It is with the hope of getting hired for a year; and their masters that are to be, farmers or others, will be seen ogling them with keen scrutiny, to find out how fit they may be for work, or worth how much wages. A scene it is not so unlike those often witnessed in your Southern States, in days happily gone by, when planters made test of the "black contraband" before buying it. The name slavery no longer darkens the statues of England; yet there is something so near akin to it in the lives of many of her poorer people that to deny its existence, *de facto*, were but a weak paltering with words.

Public dinner; from *Scenes and Characters from the Works of Charles Dickens* (London: Chapman and Hall, 1908).

XXIII.
Public Dinners.

Original publication date: September 3, 1882.

In England the Public Dinner might almost be looked upon as a National Institution, for certainly in no other country is this form of festival so conspicuous, or of such frequent occurrence. It is an adjunct, or rather central figure, to all sorts of assemblages, as Agricultural Shows, Hunt-Club Meetings, with the various anniversaries of Freemasons, Foresters and other Friendly Societies. Even sober savants, met to promote science, and philanthropists to forward the interests of charity, must have their public dinner; in short, no undertaking is deemed complete or possible without it.

From this frequency and fashion of fortifying, or gratifying, the inner man, it might be inferred that English people are well up in the gastronomic art. Yet no inference could be further from the fact. Fond of his belly, and gourmand as John Bull may be, he is aught but a *gourmet*. Indigenous cuisine he has none, or next to none; and although at his public dinners the table may groan under a sufficiency of viands, with variety as well, it is a spread at which a *chef* of the "cordon bleu" would make wry faces. True, of late years there has been improvement in this matter, but only in the large cities. In the provincial towns and rural districts public dinners are very much as of old; the bill of fare being great joints of roast and boiled—beef, veal, lamb and mutton—with hams, tongues, turkeys and fowls, also game in the season; followed by greasy puddings and tough heavy pastries. Heavy is the stomach after eating them, and needs a copious downpour of wine or other spirituous liquid to lighten it.

It is not my purpose, however, to treat of these physical

characteristics of an English public dinner, but its mental and moral ones—the idiosyncrasies which give birth to and cling around it. For it has many peculiarities, some of them ludicrously absurd; though their absurdity never seems to strike the guests themselves, nor the millions who read of their sayings and doings. Of course the *motif* of the feast has generally to do with something besides eating and drinking; the festivity itself being merely a medium to popularize some underlying interest. Oftener than otherwise it is a political one; for although the ostensible object of the dinner may be quite apart from politics, these are pretty sure to crop up in the speeches succeeding it; while the speech-makers themselves will be found at the bottom of the whole affair; they being the interested ones, either for their own profit or popularity.

It having been resolved by the wire-pullers of some association to give a public dinner, their next step is the selection and securing a chairman of high social position. If a mere parish affair the parson will do; though better the squire—if he can be had. But when it is a festival affecting a large district of country, or the whole shire, a first-class county magnate will be solicited to take the chair; a title nobleman, if such can be obtained, or, failing that, a Member of Parliament. Fitness has little or nothing to do with the choice; rank and station everything. For in England no enterprise stands much chance of success, unless under fashionable patronage. Even charity must have this, or the subscriptions to it will be few and trifling. But the list once headed by his Grace the Duke of Omnium, or the Marquis of Marigold, they will flow in with a copiousness proving how much of the milk of human kindness there is in the English heart. About the vice-chair there is not the same solicitude, it being usually occupied by the president, secretary, or some distinguished member of the association that gives the dinner, without reference to social rank. Less could not gracefully be concerned.

The repast bespoke at some hotel or tavern, and everything arranged, as the price of tickets, the list of toasts, with their proposers and seconders, the dinner comes off. Perhaps the best way to give the American reader comprehension of the after proceedings will be to adopt the newspaper report of such a dinner, or rather an epitome of it, space not allowing me to give full details, with the comments I deem it necessary to make. Let it be an Agricultural Society's dinner, as the most appropriate to a letter on English rural life. Thus said the reporter:

The dinner was given at the Green Dragon Hotel. The tables, tastefully arranged and decorated with flowers and fruit in *epergnes*, groaned under all the delicacies of the season, the *menu* being such as only Host Boniface knows how to set before his guests. The scene was enlivened by the strains of the Slopshire Volunteer Band, which played a sprightly air as the guests entered the room. Lord Thingumbob, the honored President of the Society, occupied the chair, supported on the right by Sir Barnaby Broadacres, M. P., senior member for the county, Colonel Flasher, Slopshire Volunteers, and Roger Benchley, Esq., J. P. Flanking him on the left was our popular borough member, W. Tompkins, Esq., M. P., with Major-General Greatgun, Captain Spritsail, R. N., and the Rev. Theophilus Honeytongue, vicar of Marshley-super-mud. The vice-chair was worthily filled by Mr. Holdfast, the respected treasurer of the Society, with the secretary, Mr. Scribbleton, on his right, and Mr. James Turnipfield, of Redlands Farm, on the left. The long table from top to bottom showed no gap, every seat being filled up by respectable farmers and their friends, the guests in all numbering over 100.

At this particular dinner-table, there may have been no "gap" between the seats. But I have attended more than one such festival, where there was a very marked hiatus, not for the want of guests to fill it up, but because it was deemed the correct thing to have an unoccupied space separating the "quality folk" at the table's head from the ordinary diners further down. But to continue the report:

Grace having been said by the Rev. T. Honeytongue, it is hardly necessary to state that full justice was done to the good things provided, not excepting the wines, which, from the cellars of the Green Dragon, I need not add, were of the choicest vintage.

A Victorian banquet; from the *Illustrated London News*, December 26, 1863.

The reporter omits to state how these wines of choicest vintage were set before the guests. For the information of my American readers I will supply the omission. Soon as he has uncorked a bottle, the English hotel waiter—nearest thing to a ghoul known upon earth—stands by the shoulder of him who has ordered it, with paw held half curved and an expression on his face which plainly says, "Pay, sir." Not unfrequently he makes the demand viva voce, within hearing of all; for C.O.D. is the rule of drink at most of our public dinners, just as at the bar of a liquor saloon. Then follows a groping in pockets, with a coin pulled out and passed into the palm of the white-cravated monster, who fumbles in his pocket a long while before he can find change, at length grudgingly giving it, if expected, in full. Fancy all this in the midst of a dinner, and what a damper on festivity! Were such to occur in the States, if I mistake not, the waiter would have the wine-bottle broken over his head.

PUBLIC DINNERS

The cloth having been removed, the noble chairman in a few brief but well-selected words introduced the leading toast, "Her Majesty the Queen!" which was of course responded to with universal enthusiasm. "A toast, gentlemen," he said, that needs no commendation to make it acceptable to Englishmen. We all know Her Majesty's many virtues, and that she is not only a model Queen but a model woman—everything a Royal lady should or could be. I need not say, gentlemen, how fortunate England is in being ruled by such a Sovereign; how blessed we are in having her at the head of the Nation, and how grateful all of us ought to be. Her Majesty the Queen!"

By "all of us" the noble chairman could not have meant the whole of England's people; some millions of whom, so far from being blessed by the rule of this "model Queen and model woman," are pretty badly cursed by it; the cost of keeping her and hers in barbaric luxury and splendor entailing upon them all but starvation. No thought of this, however, intruded upon the hilarity of the loyal agriculturists, at least none to hinder them from "vociferous cheering," as the reporter puts it, "all standing up, while the band played the National Anthem."

The noble chairman then gave "The Prince and Princess of Wales with the rest of the Royal Family!" "Gentlemen!" he proceeded, "it would be like telling an old story to say how every member of Her Majesty's family is endeared to all her subjects, and how popular is His Royal Highness, the Prince, our future King, with his beautiful and amiable Princess. As for the Prince himself, as you know, he is foremost in every good work; here today laying a foundation-stone; there to-morrow presiding over some charitable institution. His work is heavy, gentlemen; and the wonder is how he keeps up to it. Just now His Royal Highness has music most at heart, and is soliciting subscriptions for the establishment of a Musical College; asking the Lord-Lieutenants of counties, with the chairmen of Quarter Sessions, and the Mayors of towns, to forward this beneficial object. A Royal Prince begging alms as it were, and all for the good of his country! I trust, gentlemen, that none of you will be found wanting in appreciation of such services, or of giving the toast a warm reception." His lordship's speech elicited loud cheers, and cries of "Long live the Prince!" the guests around the table rising simultaneously and singing in chorus:

"For he's a jolly good fellow,
Which nobody can deny."

Neither Lord Thingumbob, nor the newspaper man, makes mention of the *esclandres* every now and then cropping up in connection with the name of this "jolly good fellow." Were the reporter even to allude to them, his report would not receive the honor of print' and possibly he himself, like *Othello*, might find his occupation gone. Only the most Radical of English journals ever speak of these princely escapades, and they too, with bated breath.

"Now gentleman!" proceeded the noble chairman, "charge your glasses for a toast, which I am sure all Englishmen will do full honors to. The Army, Navy and Auxiliary Forces!" Major-General Greatgun will respond for the Army, Captain Spritsail for the Navy, and our esteemed friend, Colonel Flasher, for the Auxiliary Forces."

The speeches of this trio of warriors are omitted by the reporter, who only mentions their having been made "in appropriate terms." I can give the gist of them, however; having heard and read similar ones some hundreds of times. For they are all in the same tune and strain. Like to one another as eggs to eggs. Epitomized, thus runs their gamut: "We of England are a peace-loving people, and don't wish to have war with anyone. It is to be hoped we never will have it. If it should come, however, and be forced upon us, there need be no fear but that our brave fellows, whether of the Regular Army, the Navy or the Volunteers, will give a good account of themselves." This is a subdued, modest specimen of the responding speeches to the Army and Navy toast. Often they assume the form of exalted braggadocio; and if it be a dinner where the chauvinistic Tory element is in the ascendant, like as not will be roared out that precious ditty of the "Ben Dizzy" days:

PUBLIC DINNERS

"We don't want to fight;
   But by Jingo! If we do,
We've got the ships, we've got the men,
   We've got the money too."

The ships, the men and money may be found, but how about the poor people who have to find them?

The next toast in order was "The Bishop and Clergy of the Diocese," coupled with the name of the Rev. Theophilus Honeytongue. The Reverend gentleman responded in felicitous terms, first eulogizing the Bishop—a eulogy well-deserved—then telling the assembled company how intimately their welfare was associated with that of the State and the Church. For without good government, and above all true religion, no people could be expected to prosper. Before resuming his seat the worthy vicar paid a just tribute of praise for the noble chairman, adding how thankful all of them were to his lordship for undertaking the onerous duties of the chair. (Loud and prolonged cheers.)

It is worthy of remark that the vicarial living of Marshley-super-mud is but a poor one, worth less than £200 a year, while Lord Thingumbob has several rich ones in his gift, into one of which the Reverend Theophilus may have a hope of one day getting inducted. I may also observe that sometimes at these public dinners to the toast of "Bishop and Clergy of the Diocese" is tagged "the ministers of all other denominations." But this occurs only in neighborhoods where Nonconformity is a power too strong to be slighted.

Next came the toast of The County and Borough Members, Sir Barnaby Broadacres responding for the former, and W. Tompkins, Esq., for the latter.

The loyal and patriotic toasts having been disposed of, the noble chairman called upon Roger Benchley, Esq., to propose the toast of the day, "Success and prosperity to the Slopshire Agricultural Society." IT could not have been put into better hands, and the effective speech made by the proposer, as the humorous one by Mr. Holdfast, the Society's treasurer, who responded, were highly appreciated. Toasts of a more personal nature succeeded;

the health of the noble chairman having first place. It was proposed by Mr. Turnipfield, of Redlands Farm, who in a sensible speech pointed out the debt of gratitude they all owed his lordship for condescending to preside over them on that happy festive occasion. The vice-chairman became the recipient of a similar honor, as also Mr. Scribbleton, the secretary, Farmer Turnipfield, and other distinguished members of the Society. Nor was the toast of the "The Ladies" forgotten, this being proposed by Captain Spritsail, R. N., and effectively responded to by the gallant colonel of our volunteers, Colonel Flasher. It was a late hour when the band struck up "God Save the Queen" and the company dispersed, after enjoying one of the pleasantest reunions on record.

And after "buttering one another with flattery" all over, the reporter might have added; for the amount of mutual admiration expressed at these public dinners is something marvelous—enough of it to nauseate the strongest stomach. Alike, is it with the boasting laudation of everything British, compared with which the tallest spread-eaglism of your backwoods oratory were mild and tame.

XXIV.
Farm Auction Sales.

Original publication date: September 10, 1882.

In English country life there are few occurrences more sadly suggestive than an auction-sale of farm-stock, held upon the farm. For it nearly always betokens trouble, and too often disaster and distress. At times such a sale may arise from the farm having failed to pay, and the tenant changing to another; or it may be farmer giving up agricultural pursuits altogether; in either of which cases there is nothing so greatly to be regretted about it. But as a rule the thing is otherwise, and the auctioneer's appearance upon a farmstead denotes bankruptcy, with the breaking up of the household. And the head of it may be a man not only himself born upon the farm, but whose father and grandfather before him, aye, an ancestry dating back hundreds of years and to unknown generations, were natives of the same spot. To him, his wife and their family of half-grown children, every nook and precinct of the old homestead are familiar as their own faces; the antiquated dwelling of many gables with moss-covered roof of tile, and projecting dormer windows; the walled-in "fodder," with big barn, capacious stables and cartsheds; the dove-cote where the boys have kept their pigeons; the duck-pond in which they sailed their paper boats; the orchard with its apple, pear and plum trees of ancient growth; and the rick-yard where they have romped with youthful sisters or cousins, playing hide-and-seek around huge stacks of hay and straw—all are as part of themselves. And alas! the time has come when these family joys must be abandoned, and the scenes made dear by them forsaken, perhaps never more to be revisited. For the future outlook may extend to some far distant place, likely to a land over ocean, and a new home yet to be sought for and established among strangers.

Throughout the last four or five years these breakings-up of English farmhouse homes have been painfully frequent; their frequency I need not say, being due to agricultural depression. In scarce any neighborhood has there been a week without one or more of them, as shown by the provincial newspapers, whole columns of these being often occupied by the advertisements of such sales. To the newspapers themselves it has been the reverse of a bad time; instead, a thriving profitable one, since it needs not saying that the advertisements of an auction sale, as the funeral trappings supplied by an undertaker, are charged for at highest rates. Especially is this the case when it is a bankruptcy sale, or under the too appropriately named "Law of Distress,"—that iniquitous statute which enables the landlord to pounce down upon his tenant with the suddenness of hawk upon helpless quarry, scarce any warning given. Many the poor farmers who have waked up in the morning with a belief in their being safe, if not prosperous, to see the "bums" walk boldly, even impudently, up to their doors, and present them with pieces of stamped paper; them go perambulating around their yard, and over their fields, making seizure of everything, live stock or dead. And all for a "term" or two of unpaid rent, may be only a matter of six months. It is like surrendering to a robber; but the surrender must be made, such being the law of England—a merciless, one-sided statute, enacted by her land-owning legislators, solely in their own interest. When enforced, ruin is the sure consequence, for the sale is hurried forward regardless of results, any check on haste being less due to the landlord's leniency than his fear of public reprobation; which last, however, too rarely restrains him. Knowing there will at least be a sufficiency of returns to satisfy his lien, the announcement of sale is not only informal but at shortest notices, soon to be followed by the sale itself, with everything knocked down at pitiful prices. For one reason the man thus harried might rather rejoice at the haste, and be glad to have the crisis over. For form the day of

FARM AUCTION SALES

seizure to that of settling up, a "bum" (bailiff) or "bailiff's man"—and possibly a pair of them—will have to be lodged in his house and boarded at his expense, not soliciting but saucily demanding everything of the best. One may fancy the sinister relationship between such guests—heart-hardened brutes by their very calling—and the involuntary host, with his family, themselves at such a time likely to be all but heartbroken! Alas! it is no fancy, but a reality of too common occurrence in the farmhouse homes of England.

Nor are the low prices realized at a Distress Sale all of sacrifice resultant. In addition lawyers' fees and auctioneers' charges, both on the highest scale, have to come out of the proceeds, with a further reduction for bailiff's expenses, newspaper advertising, catalogue of effects, and a host of less etceteras. No long since I took it upon myself to examine the statistics of a farm sale "under distress"; not from any curiosity, but from a belief that the farmer, beggared by it, had been scurvily treated—in fact, infamously, as I found in consulting the figures of the account rendered him. The stock upon his farm, with the household furniture, was good value for £800; yet all (sold of course under the hammer) fetched but a trifle over £300! A wagon, with the new paint little dimmed, for which only a few months before he had paid £28, went at £6, and everything else in proportion. The poor man's total of liabilities to his landlord, with all other creditors, was not quite £250; yet this forced squaring of accounts carried off his £800 worth at one fell swoop. Among the items he was debited with I found the fee of an obscure country solicitor, who could not have given more than an hour's time to the case, to be £35; and the auctioneer's charges were alike extortionate. In fat, landlord, lawyer and auctioneer, with the tribe of bailiffs and their assistants had between them, vulture like, stripped the bankrupt to his bones. Nor was it all done within the lines of the law. On scrutiny of the account, which there was some difficulty in getting tendered, I discovered an error of nearly £20 in his favor, which would never have been made good, but was evidently intended to defraud him of even this trifling residue of his wrecked fortunes. A solicitor's letter I directed to be written to the auctioneer who had charge of the sale. That, by return post, brought a check for the balance due, with profuse apologies for the "oversight." This farmer is now a broken man, and his sons working for other farmers as ordinary laborers. It is pleasant to add that they are all brave fellows, capable as uncomplaining, and as a reward for their gallant resignation to an humbler sphere of life, it is not likely to be of long continuance. Still it is sad to reflect how common these occurrence are in England—ruin due to the Law of Distress, and the helpless unfortunates harried by pettifogging lawyers and usurious money-lenders. Such cases are rife all over the land, the law courts furnishing record of only a fractional part of them.

Of farm auction sales, neither so forced nor peremptory, of course the results are less disastrous. Still there is always great sacrifice, and greater in times of depression, with money scarce in the immediate neighborhood. Even then the farmer, threatened to be stripped of everything, often bears bravely up and energetically does his best to help out the sale. This, with a sort of despairing hope it may realize something over and above his debts, though ever such a trifle—anything to begin his world anew with. For three or four weeks preceding the sale, announcement of it will appear in the local newspapers, with posters on roadside walls all over the district, giving an epitomized summary of the stock to be sold, the farm implements, and, if migration to a distant place be designed, also the house furniture. In their description none of the effects are underrated; and, to add to their attractiveness, a free luncheon will be announced by way of preliminary to the proceedings. As the auctioneer rarely raises his hammer till after 1 o'clock p.m., the eating is in good time, and generally with a good appetite. The repast is of a very substantial nature; large joints of beef and mutton, roast and boiled, with a huge ham, home cured; plenty of beer and cider served out, and the more of both drinks the better he who pays scot, and the auctioneer, will like it, for a reason easily conjectured. The spread is usually inside the dwelling-house, though at sales where the gathering is expected to be a grand one, the tables will be set in the barn, or other capacious out-building. But not all the people assembled are invited to partake; only the "respectables" and those likely to be buyers. The poor laboring man does not presume to enter inside that cheerful hall, "where beards wag all."

By the time the luncheon is over, everybody will have got upon the ground; and, perhaps, no assemblage of England's country people is so typical of her rural life as that brought together at a farm sale. There one will meet farmers of every class and kind, big ones and small ones; some prosperous and well-apparelled, others "under the weather," their seedy habiliments too plainly showing it. But not all of the crowd will be farmers; perhaps not more than half of it. The village butcher is there too, with an eye to the fat stock; the saddler, to purchase the set of plated harness, advertised as nearly "new"; the horse-dealer, after the "nag" that has worn it; with a miscellaneous host of other petty traffickers on the lookout for odds and ends.

Neither does the assemblage consist exclusively of what in England is known as the "common people"—that is the middle and lower classes. Mixed with them will be a sprinkling of the gentry, as county magistrates, clergymen and others, who have come thither with the view of securing some needed or coveted commodity at a price below the market one. Not long ago I was present at a farm-auction sale, when a baronet of my acquaintance, wealthy and of ancient lineage, bid for and bought several "odd lots," one of them a well-worn "dandy-brush" which was knocked down to him at sixpence! I mean not blame nor reproach to my titled friend by thus recording his economic action. Instead, I look upon it as altogether creditable to him; and only mention the circumstance to show the American reader that in rural England even "nobility" disdains not to be present at auction sales and pick up "bargains"—if it can.

The effects of a farm auction sale are sold *sub Jove*; generally in the orchard, or on a bit of grass pasture adjoining. Set out in array of rows will be all sorts of farming implements, lotted and labelled, with the numbers describing them in the catalogue. There will be ploughs of different patterns, single-furrow, double and boulting;—harrows, common chain and drag;—scufflers, seed-drills and rollers; horse-rakes, hay-tedding machines, chaff-cutters, oat-crushers and turnip pulpers, with many more such. Few are the English farms that are not well furnished in this way, and of the above-named implements and machines many will be in duplicate at the sale; one of best make and modern invention, the other an ancient relic of by-gone husbandry, which for a half century or more may have been out of use, kicking about, and cumbering the sheds. Four or five wagons, drawn up side-by-side, occupy a large space, some of them in good condition, others rotten and but for patching up ready to fall to pieces; all vast, ponderous vehicles, each seeming a load of itself. And so would it be to any other than the huge elephantine horses—Clydesdales and Yorkshire Punches—standing near by in the stables, or loose in the straw-yard, also this day to be sold. Two or three carts of like clumsy construction will be aligned with the wagons; then the "market trap," a light vehicle on springs, with a back supporting seat, and enough capacity rearward to carry a crate of poultry or a fatted calf. Sometimes it will be a smarter affair of the dog-cart pattern; and if the farmer in better days has been one of the very well-to-do, a pony phaeton may be also among the chattels exposed for sale. Other effects are wheelbarrows, ladders and a lawn mower; while spread out upon the grass are sets of plough and cart gearing, with the hand-tools of labor, as spades, shovels, hay-pikes, stable-forks, hedge-knives, scythes, reaping-hooks, hackers and the like, several of each lotted together. A still more miscellaneous collection are the "lots" consisting of scraps of old iron, bits of broken harness and chains, tires of wheels, ploughshares and coulters. The "marine-store dealer" from the neighboring town has come after these; and likely, having no rival in the field, he will buy them for less than the cost of carrying home.

If the sale be in one of the apple-growing shires—as Hereford, Gloucester, Worcester or Devon—there will be a turn-out of the cellar, and an exhibit of casks, as from the vaults of a wine merchant; often as many as eighty or one hundred of them. Perhaps most will be empty, though not all; some containing perry, others cider. When sold with their contents it will be at so much per gallon for the drink and so much for the cask itself. Rarely do either of these tipples fall to bring full price, or within a fraction of it, both being desirable commodities in all country places. The juice of the apple, however, is preferred to that of the pear, and commands a higher figure; the reapers and mowers saying it has more "body and bite" in it. Less fixed, or certain, is the price which the empty casks will fetch, this depending very much on the fruit-crop of that year, and somewhat, also, on the year or two preceding. If there has been a failure partially or totally, as is often the case, empty casks will be at a discount, and no one caring to bid for them. They are a bulky article, and difficult to get transported home. I have seen some of 100 gallons, their usual capacity, perfectly sound (indeed almost new), sell under the hammer for less than a dollar each, their real value being five or six times as much.

At a farm auction sale the auctioneer is not stationary, but moves from lot to lot, carrying the crowd along with him. Though not absolutely rude to one another, there is but slight show of politeness between the buyers; and in their eagerness to get a better view of the article which is "going—going," corns are trodden upon without apology. Even women are often squeezed and bustled with no "beg your pardon" heard after, if the roughly used party be a middle-aged dame of the cottager class. More courteous, even studiously polite, is the man who, every now and then, makes the round of the crowd carrying a huge jug in one hand and a tumbler in the other. Or it may be a common watering-pot and a mug; but in either case his object is to offer a free drink of whiskey-and-water to all who care to partake of it. And he will press it, too, with effusive hospitality, though his latent purpose is rather of the sinister sort. After a drink or two of the vile stuff, the lots look better and the bids range higher. Alcohol is a wonder opener of the heart; and under its influence, at these farm sales, men often make purchases which next morning they look upon with regretful grimacing.

During all the while he of the hammer keeps up a running fire of anecdote and *feux d'esprit*. Now he puts on a rueful face, tells his auditory he is actually "giving the goods away," and asks in lugubrious tone, "What will the owner say to it?" When selling a wagon, cart, or other heavy article, reproachfully deploring the low bids he will exclaim, "Why gentlemen! it's worth all that to break up for firewood or the old iron!" Many of these country auctioneers are really humorous, much more so than those of the large cities, though much less is their humor appreciated—if it be at all fine. The English farmer is rather a dull auditor, though now and then a broad joke will draw him into laughter. He grows jollier after the whiskey jug has gone several times round; but, take it all in all, the farm auction sale is anything but a hilarious affair.

When it is over, the lighter and less bulky lots purchased will be taken home by the purchasers in their "traps." Most of the live-stock, too, will be driven off; but not till the next morning or evening is there a complete dismantling. Then all outdoor effects will be removed, and the barn, stable, cowhouse, sheds and piggeries left empty.

The furniture is usually sold on a later day, perhaps a week intervening. Then the Household Gods [sic] have to go too, all sacrificed, save, perhaps, a few of the more cherished ones, that may have been saved from the keen eyes of the creditor. In fine, the old farmhouse stands un-tenanted or left to a caretaker; they who hitherto inhabited it, maybe all their lives, gone clear away, few knowing wither, and still fewer caring.

Dock scene in England; from *The Graphic*, August 8, 1874.

XXV.
The Best Sort of Englishman for America.

Original publication date: September 17, 1882.

Since my letters to you on England's sham of Parliamentary representation, an article has appeared in the *The Nineteenth Century* touching on the same subject. The writer exclaims: "Heaven preserve England, and make her public men think what will become of their country, not what will become of themselves, at the next election. If the state of the Irish question is bad and dangerous, equally bad, and fraught with still greater danger, is the state of the House of Commons. On the Irish question itself the action of Parliament is paralyzed, not only by the presence in the national council of the delegates of the rebellion, from Ireland, but by the influence which, thanks to that masterpiece of profligacy, the Reform Bill of 1867, is now exercised over a number of members for English constituencies by the votes of the Irish, who are congregated in the great centres, and there invested with political power, while the British laborer, an incomparably better citizen, remains unenfranchised in the scenes of his patient toil. But the Parliamentary anarchy is not confined to the Irish question. The House of Commons is fast becoming a chaos. As to the House of Lords, it objects are those of a narrow class, and in pursuing them it only increases the confusion…but how can the strong and wise man be picked out and summoned to the scene of action? The man would have to go through a party election in which he would stand a very poor chance against a stump orator or a long purse."

Having only read this article in a newspaper that had copies it, and without the author's name appended, I know not who he is. But I need not say that most writers who have admission to the columns of *The Nineteenth Century* are men of mark, and supposed to be well acquainted with what they write about. So far, therefore, this writer confirms what I said of the House of Commons, almost echoing my words, some of which I may be permitted to here reproduce: "One would naturally expect that a candidate for Parliamentary honors would be required to give some proof of his fitness for Parliamentary duties...No such qualification is needed...Political capacity and knowledge of statesmanship—or indeed other knowledge of any useful kind—are the least and last things thought of. Money will make them take the wall...A man without money, or of only moderate means, aspiring to Parliament is a thing never thought of. Such a man never thinks it of himself...Even the preliminary expenses of election are sufficiently deterrent; and what must accrue after, whether elected or rejected, will further impoverish if not totally ruin him."

It is not the rivalry of the stump orator, however, that the poor but legitimate aspirant to a seat in the House of Commons need fear. The phrase, which *The Nineteenth Century* writer has borrowed from your side, has but little application to England; neither has the thing itself; and they who enter Parliament by such an influence are few compared with the men of long purses. To an English constituency, no amount of eloquence, stump or otherwise,—even with statesmanship capacity to back it,—is so convincing as the chink and jingle of gold. That is the best key for opening the door of England's House of Commons. With regard to the British laborer remaining unenfranchised in the scenes of his patient toil, I said: "Were these non-voters less intelligent, or less politically enlightened, that those endowed with the franchise, there might be some excuse for its being withheld from them. But such is not the case; instead rather the opposite, most of them being quite as capable of a rational and beneficial exercise of it as those who do exercise it, and many of them more."

The chief reason assigned for denying participation in government to the poor laborer, and giving it all to the rich or those owning property, is that only the latter have a "stake in the country" and therefore alone entitled to administer its affairs. This hoary saw and child of sin,—a relic of ancient feudalism,—is preached on platforms day after day; a sort of knock-down argument dinned into the ears of unreflecting ignorance, till it has almost come to be looked upon as an axiom. Yet never was doctrine or dogma further from the truth; indeed it is the very reverse of it. For what stake can a man have in any country greater or more precious than his life and his life's happiness, with that of his family? And by what natural right should the control of these be the exclusive privilege of the rich, any more than of the poor? Indeed, if a difference in political power were a thing to be thought of, would seem but fair that the larger portion of it should be conceded to the poor man, as a compensation for his less measure of enjoyment socially.

Such questions, however, are foreign to the purpose of the present letter, which is to give the American people a hint that may interest and I hope be of service to them; and as it more especially concerns the American farmer. THE TRIBUNE seems the very medium for conveying it. My suggestion is that the men most wanted on your side, the most likely to benefit you in a National sense, are these same poor laborers, the unenfranchised of England. This may not be general belief; indeed, the opposite would seem to prevail, judging from what I read in your newspaper. These, recording the arrival of immigrants now and then indulge in gratulation about the newcomers being of a class above that of the laborer, and all the warmer are they welcomed if in fine attire, with £100 or £200 in pocket, as it were bringing so much grist to the mill. But what of this? What signifies such a paltry entrance-fee compared with the bone and sinew of a man well able for work, and eagerly willing to do it, even though he present himself in corduroys and with empty scrip? A single year, or at most a couple, will equalize the values of the two kinds of immigrants; after which the advantages will be all against the petty capitalist, and on the side of the proletarian, not only to himself but to the country of his adoption. I do not say that this holds true universally, but only as a rule; for as a rule he with the hundred odd pounds has neither work in him, nor the design of doing it. If a farmer, he will be of the sort who took things too easily at home; hence his having to leave it. The same with his sons and daughters' the latter, in all likelihood, better acquainted with the piano than the milkpail; while the capabilities of the former were not long ago described to me by a farm laborer, saying: "Sir, they don't know a plough's head from its tail." It is an absolute fact that very few English farmers' daughters can make either butter or cheese of commendable quality, and fewer still understand the management of poultry. The former industries are usually left to the "maid-of-all-work"; the latter to the cottage dame, wife of the laboring man, who knows and does the business better. And just as with the daughters, so with the sons; these often devoting more of their time to "Tally-ho" than to the raising of stock or the culture of crops. And it is the same all over England. Were it otherwise the number of her farmers now seeking homes in your country would be infinitely less, or *nil*, and perhaps to your advantage. For they are not the best sort to aggrandize any nation, in an economic sense, and far less politically. Mostly of the Tory type, ingrained in their hearts is the belief in monarchy, with no end of narrow-minded national prejudices, which they will be slow to cast off, if they ever should. Besides, with most of them, it is less the thought of leading an industrious life than an easy, idle one that guides to their emigration.

With the laboring man it is different—indeed the reverse. His leanings are neither monarchical nor national; for how could he care for a system of government he knows to be his bane, or a country of which he is in no sense a citizen? Circumstances force him to acknowledge them, but it is with a less patient than surly protest, and a readiness to rebel should opportunity offer. Just on this account is the man to embrace republicanism, and cling to it with a true, loving faith, as that which has given him his first throb of freedom and happiness, with his first step along the path of prosperity. Therefore have I ventured on giving the hint that he is your man for America. There may be some of your people who will say they neither want him nor any other, and that you have had enough of immigration. But I take it, they who think thus are few in number, and that the craze of "Native Americanism" has long since ceased to afflict you. It was not only an injustice but a delusion; and moreover a suicidal one to the deluded. No people has a natural right to place boundaries, and bar up any portion of the earth's surface against outsiders, or withhold from them the privilege of citizenship, should they care to claim it, and show credentials without taint of criminality. Jealousy exclusivism will dwarf the growth and stint the resources of the most favored nation, by forcing it, as it were, to feed upon itself. For the larger the population of a country—provided it be a free country—the better it is for every individual inhabitant of it, and the man who does not know this must have read the lessons of history with scales upon his eyes. I fancy there are not many such on your side of the Atlantic, though on this nearly all are so. Incredible as it may seem, there is hardly an Englishman, even of those called statesmen, who does not believe that to get rid of these poor proletarians—surplusage of population, as they conceive it—it is a national gain, and a thing to be thankful for!

Under such circumstance it might be supposed that you could have as many of these little-appreciated and ill-rewarded toiler, as you care to take. And so you can, by making an effort, for an effort would be needed. You don't get them now in any great numbers, a variety of obstructions standing in the way of their reaching you. First, there is the difficulty of their finding their way unpiloted, another the far greater one from their being unassisted. For, to repeat what I said in my letter about the farm laborer, his paying passage across the Atlantic—even the lowest-priced steerage, and even but for himself, without thought of wife or children—were the next thing to an impossibility. It would take years of toil, and cheese-paring economy, with the patience of Job and the resolution of Hercules, to accomplish it.

But there is still another obstructive cause against the farm-laborer going your way; which is, that he is guided in a different direction. However little cared for at home, he is in demand and competed for in English colonies. Canada stretches forth her hand to clutch him, and still longer arms are extended, with like aim, from Australia and New Zealand. England makes every effort to send him to one colony or the other; for it is a great chagrin to the "Chauvinistic" Britisher to see his flag forsaken, even by those to whom he behaves so badly. Withal, he shows stinginess in adding this sort of immigration—even with the help sent by the other side—only partially franking passages, and under conditions that render the enterprise little attractive. Of late a grand spurt of pretended philanthropy had led to a large draught of laborers getting carried free to Canada, and on to Manitoba. But, if I mistake not, most them in time find their way to a country further south, and well for them if they do.

That you want more of this farm-laborer element in the States, I have reason to know; having received several letters from unknown though not anonymous correspondents on your side, inquiring of me how, and what way, they might secure such valuable "helps." As most of the writers appear to be farmers, and all readers of THE TRIBUNE, I crave your permission to answer them as one, formulating my reply as follows: You cannot get the best class of English farm-laborers without some enterprise on your part. It will need his passage to be wholly, or partially, paid for him, with contract for a fixed term of service, and amount of wages stipulated. Then, on his part there should be agreement to forego receipt of wages till the passage money, or any other expenses be recouped to his employer; after which he should be free to go elsewhere, if it pleases him. To make all this effective, it would be necessary to establish an understanding in mutual good faith. The laborer should know all about the situation offered him, so as to judge whether it be worthy of his acceptance; and he who offers it must be assured of getting the sort of man he has bargained for; above all, that the advanced money will be honestly returned in work. In these conditions lies the chief difficulty; though there seems a way of overcoming it. The thing might be done on the cooperative principle; by the establishment of a syndicate on your side, with sufficient capital to meet the transport expenses of the engaged immigrants. On this side the necessity would be an agent, or agents, of known name and integrity, to give confidence to the intending immigrant, as also to make sure of his being "the right man for the right place"; otherwise rejecting him. If such arrangement could be made, I have little doubt but that many an English farm-laborer would be glad to avail himself of it; and still less doubt of his finding it to his advantage, as likely also would the man who employs him.

Naturalist Field Club meeting; from the Illustrated London News, September 23, 1865.

XXVI.
Naturalists' Field Clubs and Archæological Societies.

Original publication date: September 24, 1882.

An account of English country life not including the learned associations whose titles form the heading of this article, would be incomplete. For, although their headquarters may be in towns, most of the members belonging to them are residents of the country, and there, with little exception, lies the scene of their operations. The exception is with the archaeological societies; the "Naturalists' Field Club," as its title imports, being strictly a rural institution; and to it will this letter be more especially devoted.

I take it, you have similar associations in the United States; but probably neither so numerous nor so well-organized. Indeed, it is not likely that in any country are so many of them as in England, since in no other are the conditions so favorable to their existence. The naturalist and archaeologist may have as good a field elsewhere, or even better; but the explorers of it are fewer, if not altogether wanting. In England they abound; a fact that may appear creditable to England, as evincing a high degree of culture, or at least aspirations to and pursuit of scientific knowledge. Probed to the bottom, however, it will be found to rest on a basis not quite so laudable, though still commendable, the real explanation being that in rural England there are some thousands of educated, or semi-educated, men—for it is the *cult* of Oxford and Cambridge—who have scarce anything to do except kill time in one way or another. The majority of these gentlemen of "elegant leisure" are clergymen, incumbents of country parishes, and as the color of their cloth is a bar—though not always—to the faster field sports of hunting and shooting, they betake themselves to the more

THE RURAL LIFE OF ENGLAND

refined and greater enjoyment of Naturalists' Field Clubs.

That in these their numbers predominate, I may offer as example the one to which I myself belong—the "Woolhope." It takes its title from that remarkable and symmetric upheaval of Silurian rocks in the parish of Woolhope Herefordshire, the study and correlation of whose fossils laid the foundation of Sir Roderick Murchison's fame. It was not he, however, who correlated them, or at least not altogether, the better part of the work being done by an obscure country clergyman named Lewis, a true geologist, who generously imparted his discoveries to the author of "Siluria,"[8] modestly waiving all credit for himself, and never receiving it. I have often heard Murchison called an empiric; certainly his scientific fame is far above his deservings, and Mr. Lewis might well say of his own filched honors:

"Hos ego versiculos feci, tulit alter honorem."[9]

But to return to Naturalists' Field Clubs. Looking over the list of the "Woolhope's" members, I find there are 150 of them, nearly a third of whom are clergymen. There are a lord, and two or three baronets; a couple of members of Parliament; a sprinkling of Army and Navy officers (retired from service); half a dozen doctors; and the remainder gentlemen, many of whom are county magistrates, and all either by legal entitlement or courtesy having "Esq." appended to their names. No, not all. I had almost omitted to state that three or four names appear in the list with the simple prefix, "Mr." and so in all reports of proceedings, whether it be of the club's meetings and dinners, or the papers read thereat. The plain Misters are men engaged in trade, and though in scientific

---

[8] This is a reference to Reid himself, who wrote a manuscript, "The Naturalist in Siluria," while residing at Frogmore, in Herefordshire. It was posthumously published in 1890.
[9] This is a quote from Vergil, which roughly translates to ""I wrote the verse, another filched the praise."

attainments the equals indeed some of them the superiors, of their fellow members, the titular distinction—invidious, I may also call it—is rigidly adhered to. In England even science, natural or other, is afflicted with ideas of social precedence and snobbery.

By the above it will be seen that the aristocratic element enters largely into the composition of Naturalist Field Clubs. But, I may observe, that in this respect the "Woolhope" has rather a preeminence; though in most others a majority of the members are of the gentry class, and in nearly all every third or fourth member is a clergyman. I have no statistics at hand enabling me to give the exact number of these clubs throughout the kingdom; but roughly stating it, there must be two or three hundred of them. Most counties have one, some two; and in the thickly populated northern shires, the centres of manufacturing industry, some towns have their Naturalist clubs. These are of a less aristocratic character; their members being mostly young men in the middle ranks of life, with praiseworthy aspirings.

Of course the Naturalists' Field Club has headquarters, usually in the county town, though no always. Some other may be more central, and affording equally as good, or better, accommodations. But as the indoors work is of little consequence compared with that done out-doors, office-rent, clerkage and such like expenses are not very onerous. The chief items on the debit side related to the printing of circulars, and the "Transactions," with binding the latter, and postage; while to credit stand the subscriptions of the members, with the entrance fees of those who may have joined during the year. Taking the statistics of the "Woolhope," which may be looked upon as a fair sample, the entrance fee is 10 shillings, or $2.50, and the annual subscription the same, the whole amount of yearly receipts and disbursements being under £100. This, however, does not include the rent of offices; as, by the munificence of one of its members, the club has quarters in a fine building rent free. The expense of attending the field meetings is another matter; but, of course, such attendance is voluntary. The officers of the club are a president, vice-president, secretary, treasurer and committee of management; all annually elected and all unpaid.

There are six meetings in the year; one of them termed the "annual meeting," which is held late in February or March. It is an indoors affair, at which the chief business of the club is transacted, the annual accounts audited, officers chosen for the year, and the days for the field-meetings fixed, as also the places. These all occur in the summer months—between May and October—after which there is nothing more heard of Naturalists' Field Clubs, that, throughout the winter, like dormice, seem to be asleep.

When the day for a field meeting draws nigh, each member receives a circular from the secretary, reminding him of it; also making known the place, the best means of reaching it, and where the dinner is to be. Always that dinner! The British savant could not discuss science without it. In fixing the place of a field meeting there is an eye to its adaptability for instruction or exploration; enjoyment of scenery is also a factor in the case. At one time it will be the ascent of some noted mountain, at another inspection of any ancient Roman camp or visit to a ruined castle or abbey. For, notwithstanding the exclusive specialty of their title, archaeology is a prevailing element in Naturalists' Field Clubs. Not so much as geology, however; this in most of them being the predominant feature' and, as a consequence, the places of meeting are often where the "lore of the rocks" can be best studied. For the same reason, the scenery will be picturesque, so giving a double advantage. But, *per contro*, it will generally also be difficult to get at; and to facilitate reaching it means of transport have to be arranged, and provided beforehand. As a rule the railway authorities are accommodating to field clubs, and will not only put on a special train for the excursionists, but often improvise a sort of platform station convenient as possible to the point aimed at. When this is so distant from the railway as to daunt pedestrians, then common road conveyances have to be chartered; also a matter of prearrangement. The secretary's circular tells where they will be in waiting, and states the price per head for transport to and fro. On such occasions will be seen a string of vehicles wending its way along some lone country road, a miscellaneous assortment of private carriages transformed into "flys," wagonettes, dog-carts and even farmers' market traps; all jam full, not a seat unoccupied, and with a freight that makes the rustics stare in wonder. Belike they have never witnessed such a procession, or seen so many odd looking gentlemen together; certainly never so many "parsons"; for at field meetings the clerical element musters more than usually strong, often outnumbering the lay.

A spectacle equally unique will be witnessed shortly after; though it may occur beyond ken of the ordinary spectator; being in a place remote from human habitation. On the summit of a mountain, or the *agger* of an ancient camp, the same assemblage of gentlemen, now gathered into a group, some seated, some reclining on the grass, as they listen to the "field address" delivered by one of their number. If on a mountain, this will be geologic, and the speaker, seen now facing this way, now that, as he points out a line of cliffs indicating the presence of carboniferous limestone, or to a bold hill projection that tells of an outpouring of trap, or basalt, which has hindered denudation of the softer sedimentary rock underneath, and so preserved the hill. If time permit, there will be other addresses given, or papers read, and on a variety of subjects. As a rule, however, the journey thither, with that due on return home, makes time precious, and the unread papers are "taken as read," to appear in the printed "Transactions," if judged worthy. Besides there is some field botanizing and practical geologizing yet to be done, and after the dinner; this with many of the excursionists not the lease important event of the day. So in good time there is a breaking up of the assemblage into several smaller groups, who stroll about in different directions, some with grabbing trowel and vasculum in search of rare species of ferns or other uncommon plants, and some armed with the orthodox geological hammer in the hope of laying bare a fossil. Should there be a quarry convenient, the geologists will find their way to it; when a very fusillade or cracking and chipping follows, to the astonishment and often amusement of the quarrymen Any remarkable ruin the neighborhood will be visited, as also the parish church. And here the local archæologist—usually the rector or vicar himself—takes conduct of the excursionists and inflicts upon them his limited acquaintance with the past, architectural and otherwise. Every pane of stained window glass, every memorial table against wall or in the flagged floor, with carvings of altar and rood-screen, is dilated upon with as much earnest volubility as though it were knowledge worth attaining, while in point of fact it is scarce worth a word. The amount of the fiddle-faddle about old churches, and the *reliquiæ* of past times generally, is something to be surprised at; though the craze—for such I cannot help calling it—is not confined to Englishmen; instead seems even more a madness with Americans.

In the case of the Naturalists' Field Club this church dissertation is not always listened to with remarkable patience. For by this time the excursionists have become hungry, and dinner is the prevailing idea. So there will be sounding of the President's call-whistle and a quick rallying around him of the scattered and straying groups. Then a hurried return to where the chartered conveyances have been left, a scrambling into seats, and back to the place of departure. This will be the village inn—whose Boniface has not only provided the carriage transport but the dinner, of course also "bespoke." A substantial repast, and fairly good; at all events appreciated. After mountain climbing, with long fasting, the diners are not disposed to cavil at the cookery, or the viands being cold, as most of them are. To furnish a hot dinner for so many guest would overtask the capabilities of the village hostelry. Moreover, the meal has to be eaten hurriedly, with all ears on the alert, dreading at each instant to hear the screech of railway whistle, announcing the train at the station. For that train may be the last of the day, and should they fail to catch it, then a dilemma indeed. So there is no time for speechifying or toasts save one: "Her Majesty the Queen," which is never omitted. It must not, dare no, else science would be deemed disloyal. The dinner is so much per head, each paying for his own. Three shillings and sixpence is the customary charge, stipulated for by the club's committee and set forth in the secretary's circular. This, of course, does not include wine or other drink; which if ordered is paid for by him who orders it, then and there. The table-waiter, it may be the landlord himself—expects "cash down upon the nail," as at most other public dinners in England.

Many of those who attend field-meetings may not belong to the club. By the rules each member has the privilege of bringing a friend with him; and although ladies are not officially members, a few will be present at most field meetings. But there is one in every year specially devoted to the feminine element, termed the Ladies' Day, on which they appear in overpowering numbers. Nor need I say that at this particular meeting the gentlemen turn up more numerous than usual; many of them thinking it the real enjoyable event of the year; though the zealous naturalists take a different view of the matter, and would grumble at it—if they dared. For on the Ladies' Day it is nearly all pic-nic, and but little of science teaching.

The modes and ways of Archæological Societies do not greatly differ from those of Naturalists' Field Clubs, save in their exclusive devotion to the one study from which they taken their name. They are also fewer in numbers; and, as already said, less of a rural institution than the Naturalists' Field Clubs, though most of their meetings are also amid country scenes.

To sum up, I should say that Naturalists' Field Clubs are not only laudable in aim, but of good service in their action. In England they have done much to develop natural science, and to the public benefit. Especially is this true in regard to geology; a branch of knowledge until lately looked upon as mere theoretical speculation, but now known to be a factor of most practical value, if only as an aid to mining operations. As proof and illustration of this, I may adduce a somewhat comical incident that occurred, but a short while ago near my own neighborhood, though it proved anything but a comedy to the hero of it. He was a gentleman owning a tract of land, under which he imagined there was coal, and employed a number of working miners to dig for it. They sank shafts hundreds of feet deep, and tunnelled away for weeks and months—in short, till their employer's exchequer became empty, and he could no longer meet their wage demand. As the story goes, these subterraneous searchers, day after day, brought up from the bowels of the earth and made a parade of "chunks" of coal, the genuine thing itself. Yet were their sinkings through strata of the Devonian, or old red sandstone, rocks in geologic order thousands of feet below where coal could possibly be found, and whose deposition occurred, no knowing how many millions of years, before coal had existence on the earth.

The merest tyro in geology could have told this foolish man what an *ignis fatuus* he was pursuing. And he was told it, but to no purpose. With mule-like obstinacy or rather mole-like persistency, he kept tunnelling on, till the evil day came, and his estate tumbled into bankruptcy.

Failure of the English Hay Crop

Original publication date: August 7, 1882

CAPTAIN MAYNE REID DESCRIBES THE WIDESPREAD RUIN WROUGHT BY PROTRACTED RAINS—LOSSES AMOUNTING TO MANY MILLIONS OF DOLLARS

To the Editor of the Tribune.

SIR: IN THE TRIBUNE of July 2 I note a paragraph commencing thus: "The English farmers are threatened with the ruin of the hay-crop, owing to cold and rainy weather." I regret to inform you that the threat has been fulfilled, and the ruin has come, almost wholesale and complete. No doubt this intelligence has long since reached you by the forestalling cable; still it may interest your readers to learn the particulars of the calamity—for a calamity it is. In England two kinds of hay are made—one from clover, commonly called "fodder"; the other, or hay proper, being the product of field and meadow grass. In quantity the former is much less than the latter, probably only a fourth or fifth of the whole crop. As the clover is earlier ready for the scythe, nearly all of it was mown by the middle of June, or a little later. But scarce was it down when a spell of rain set in, continuing intermittently for more than a week, so that nothing could be done with it. Luckily there succeeded an interval of fine weather,—three or four days of it,—when by quick work the fodder was got into the rickyard, too hastily, however, and as a consequence it is ill-conditioned, where not altogether spoiled. During these dry days the mowers were again active, and down went the meadow grass all over the land; at least three-fourths of it having been cut by the 1st of July. But on the evening of that day the rain recommenced, and has been pouring down ever since; of course not continuously, but in showers too closely successive for the curing of hay. In the moist climate of the British Isles desiccation is slow compared with that of your dry elastic atmosphere; and as for the last three weeks we have had rain every day, with only one exception, I need not say that the cut grass is still upon the ground, rotting and rotted. It is raining while I write (July 20) with no appearance of a dry spell likely to be permanent. But it matters not much now; for even if fine weather were to come this day or to-morrow, it will come too late. Most of the hay is already gone, not to the rickyard but to ruin, and I hear of large quantities being hauled to the manure-heap.

The result cannot fail to be lamentable; for the loss must be great. Indeed, a national loss; though, from what I read in the newspapers, the nation does not appear as yet fully to realize it. Guided by agricultural statistics, in rough estimate I make it out to be not less than £10,000,000, though it may prove nearer £20,000,000. In Great Britain and Ireland there are 19,000,000 acres of grass-land and clover. Taking half of this acreage as pasture, with half kept for hay, and valuing the latter at £5 per acres, we get nearly £50,000,000 worth of it. If, then, a third, or even a fourth of this be lost, as I believe one or other will be,—indeed, now is,—what a gap it will make in the industrial receipts of the year, and what an emptiness in the pockets of the farmers, to say nothing of how their stock must suffer through the winter to come! But half recovered from many blows of adversity late given them, this new one will send them staggering back, no doubt devoting some of themselves to ruin, as their hay.

The paragraph in your paper from which I quoted had reference to an invention for "drying hay in the stack," lately much talked of her. The plan is being experimented upon; but so far the results are dubious, and anything but hopeful. Indeed, it is already spoken of as a failure. Yours,

MAYNE REID

Frogmore, Ross, Herefordshire, July 20, 1882.

www.ingramcontent.com/pod-product-compliance
Lightning Source LLC
Chambersburg PA
CBHW070144100426
42743CB00013B/2815